Imagine Loving Your Work

imagine
Loving Your Work

A Woman's Guide
to the Career Puzzle

Marti Chaney with Vicki Thayer

CELESTIAL ARTS
BERKELEY, CALIFORNIA

The exercise that begins on page 112 is used with permission of Hilda Lee Dail, Ph.D., from *The Lotus and the Pool,* Shambala Publications, Inc. © 1983, 1989.

Cover design by Fifth Street Design
Text design by Sarah Levin
Typesetting by Star Type

FIRST CELESTIAL ARTS PRINTING 1993

Library of Congress Cataloging-in-Publication Data

Chaney, Marti.
    Imagine loving your work : a woman's guide to
the career puzzle / by Marti Chaney & Vicki Thayer.
        p.   cm.
    ISBN 0-89087-701-7 : $12.95
    1. Vocational guidance for women—United
States. 2. Women—Employment—United States.
3. Inner child. 4. Self-actualization
(Psychology) I. Thayer, Vicki. II. Title
HF5382.65.C48   1993   93-32108
331.7'02'082—dc20   CIP

1 2 3 4 5 6 7 8 / 99 98 97 96 95 94 93

Marti dedicates this book:

To the women who have been and are now a part
of my life. Through their actions and words, they
have taught me to live with strength, integrity,
warmth, humor, and passion.

Vicki dedicates this book:

To my mother, Mildred Thayer; to my grandmother,
Eva Wilson; and to the other women of my family
who provided my first lessons about women
working and living their potential.

Table of Contents

Acknowledgments

To Marti and Vicki's families, associates, clients, friends, and co-workers who listened, completed surveys, answered questions, shared their experiences, tested exercises and activities, and believed in us and our book throughout the process: We would like to thank you for your invaluable help and inspiration in the completion of *Imagine Loving Your Work*.

We offer David Hinds, Veronica Randall, Alexis Brunner, and the rest of the Celestial Arts staff our unfailing devotion and greatest respect for their expertise, support, and guidance in this project. They've made it fun, and almost painless, to edit the book, and easy to love the publishing process.

...then the day came when the risk
to remain tight in a bud
was more painful than the risk
it took to blossom.

ANÄIS NIN

CHAPTER 1

Introduction:
Is Something
Missing?

L ife's too short to stay in a crummy job. And you can quote us on that. We want to help you enjoy your life to its fullest. The time and energy expended on our career is a big chunk of what we do during our life. Since we spend so much time there, we feel work should be fun and fulfilling, challenging and exciting. We see work as an integral part of our whole lives, not just a place we spend a portion of our day.

How Did this Book
Come to Be?

Our purpose in writing a career guide is to help you find that sense of fulfillment in what you do. If you feel like you are in a crummy job, or are just vaguely dissatisfied, but feel like things should be better, or you want more out of your work, then this book is written for you.

When you are satisfied with your career, you feel good about yourself.

Your interactions with other people are more positive. And when you feel good, what you produce is of a better quality; not only at work, but at home and in your relationships as well. It has a "rippling" effect in all aspects of your life.

If you're not sure this is true, think back to a time when you had a job that you loved. What was your life like? You probably felt happy, confident, competent, in control, energized. Now consider a time when you were in a job you disliked. It was a whole different experience, wasn't it?

Days spent in jobs that don't fit who we are can seem to last forever. We become clock-watchers. We are often cranky and short-tempered with our peers and this sometimes can spill over at home. When we choose to work at a job we hate, it also erodes our self-confidence. We may find ourselves plagued by feelings of fear and self-doubt.

This guide will help you find a career that matches who you really are. Work is a part of how we express ourselves, and it should be a joyful, affirming activity in our lives. Since we are constantly growing and changing, we need to constantly re-evaluate what we are doing and consider the need for change in our lives.

Clients often come to career counseling feeling that "something is missing." As they work through their career decision-making process, they discover that clues about what is missing often can be found in their childhood. The things they loved to do, the likes and dislikes that they had as children, the games they liked to play and pretend all contain valuable information about who they really are now. Discovering this wealth of childhood information, making contact with that part of ourselves, provides invaluable information, and by incorporating it into one's work, leads to greater career and personal satisfaction. Our book is designed to help you make that same journey of self-discovery and integration.

The process has worked for others, and it can also work for you. We know hundreds of clients who have made changes in their lives as a result of integrating their childhood dreams into their work. You will read some of their stories in the following chapters.

The terms "career," "job," and "work" are used interchangeably in this book. While everyone has a personal definition of these words, we define them by saying that they represent getting paid for what is best about you, for being who you are. We believe that work, career, or job is a means of self-expression, a tangible manifestation of who we are. As you see these three terms used throughout the book, we urge you to keep this definition in mind. These three words mean far more to us than a paycheck.

We believe that one's life, and career, function better when we are engaged in what we were meant to do, living the life we were meant to live. We both put into practice what we believe, and both of us use the process outlined here to build our own career satisfaction.

Our collaboration on this career guide has included all the steps we will be sharing with you. Writing this book has been fun, challenging, fulfilling, rewarding, and occasionally overwhelming! We hope that your experience in reading and using *Imagine Loving Your Work* will be as positive as our experience of developing it has been.

Why Is this Book Right for You?

Deciding what you want to be when you grow up can be a confusing process. It can be so difficult that many of us still have not reached a decision by the time we reach our 20s, or 40s, or 60s. Sometimes we feel pulled in many directions, perhaps torn between what we feel we have to do to support ourselves and what we dream about being able to do, "if we only could."

Our methods will help facilitate your move from career confusion to career clarity. They are designed to guide you through a personal journey of discovery—about who you are, about what you like, about what you are good at, about what you have to offer the workplace, and about what you want from your career. Consider this book a personal journal of the steps you will take to discover the clues to achieving career satisfaction.

You will follow a reconnection process, linking yourself with the inner child part, as a way to find clues about what you want from your career. Actually, you'll find it rewarding to reclaim that part of yourself and to remember the joyful, delightful child you once were—the one who lives within you still!

"Inner Child" Work

There has been a great deal written about the "inner child," particularly in healing the effects of the dysfunctional family. For many, this work is very necessary and important. For the purpose of this book, however, we are focusing not on the traumatic aspect of the inner child. Rather, we ask that you recall the positive and happy child you were, filled with interests, talents and abilities that make you unique.

Doing the exercises in this book and spending time with your inner child may indeed bring up unpleasant memories, especially if you were raised in a dysfunctional family. If you experience particularly uncomfortable and sad, or extremely traumatic memories, we encourage you to seek counseling or other support for dealing with those critical issues.

We believe that it is important for you to find the positive support that your wounded child inside needs in order to heal and grow. However, our book is not designed to help you resolve those kinds of issues. We are focusing on the positive experiences of your natural child and how those experiences can relate to your career choices and overall life-work satisfaction. When, and if, you come upon a negative in your work with this process, pause a minute and re-focus. Say to yourself, "I acknowledge that this memory (or feeling) is here, but now is not the time to take care of it. I will..." Then, make a promise to yourself about how and when you will take care of these memories and feelings.

On the Trail of a Clue

As you become a "detective" with the natural child part of yourself, you will find clues that help you to:

➤ Know Yourself—by discovering the unique person you really were and really are.

➤ Know Your Beliefs—by examining the work heritage passed down from your family and from society.

➤ Value Yourself—by appreciating the skills, talents, qualities, and abilities you have.

➤ Honor Yourself—by finding work that not only "fits" you and meets your values, needs, and desires but that also expresses your individuality.

You will gather these clues and structure them to develop a concrete plan for finding career satisfaction. As Lily Tomlin said, "I always wanted to be somebody, but I guess I should have been more specific." The plan of action you will develop through this book will provide you with a specific, detailed map to follow in reaching your career destination.

Tips for Using
Imagine Loving Your Work

Give yourself some credit. You have taken the first step on a journey that many people never make. Using this book shows that you are interested in and committed to learning more about yourself and making changes in your life. This involves risking and taking a chance. It is not always easy, so take your time and reward yourself frequently. Congratulations! You are on your way!

This work is a personal journey, but you needn't make it alone. You are unique. Your journey to career satisfaction will be like no one else's.

It can be helpful, however, to work with others who are also searching for their own career satisfaction clues. Perhaps you will want to form a team or start a class with others who are using this guide. Maybe you would prefer to work with a friend or career counselor, one-on-one. Finding others to work with can provide you with support and structure.

Colleagues are also valuable when you desire feedback or want help sorting out the thoughts and ideas that will surface.

We urge you to seek out others who are positive and supportive of your career search process. Sometimes those who are closest to us, our family and loved ones, are not necessarily the best source of this support. Perhaps they feel unhappy about their own work situation, or they may view your change process as threatening.

Remember to choose support team members who are also committed to creating a better career future for themselves. Choose career counselors who love their work, so that they can be supportive in helping you to love yours. Create the kind of team that will help you to win!

Make our methods work for you. All of us have different learning styles. That means that we process information in various ways. We have included a variety of activities designed to help you learn more about yourself.

However, you may find some of the exercises and activities of more value to you personally than others. Please pick and choose the ones you wish to complete. Perhaps you would rather draw a picture than write a response to some of the questions. By all means, do it! Let your creativity surface and trust your intuition as well.

No, you can't flunk these exercises, unless you are "grading" yourself. There are no "right" answers to your personal journey. There is no one giant "career truth" that will swoop down from the heavens and thunder through your subconscious. And, most importantly, there is no need to judge yourself and feel guilty about what you have or haven't done for yourself in the past.

Having fun is an important part of your journey through this process. Use colored pencils or pens, draw your pictures in crayon, cut and paste, use glitter. Play and have a good time. Adapt the activities to meet your needs as you uncover information that has likely been locked away for many years. The important part is the outcome. What you want to achieve at the end of your journey is greater career and personal satisfaction. Keep your destination in mind and direct your efforts toward this goal.

Please take special note: We recommend that you read the chapters in order. Because working toward your plan is a building process, the information in each chapter builds on that shared in the previous one.

You can certainly take your time. You will find that this is a guide best read and applied over the course of many evenings or weekends. Completing the exercises is a thoughtful kind of work. Set aside time for this creative, exciting, and helpful process—you deserve it!

And, finally, give yourself permission to relax, have fun, and proceed at your own pace. Your journey may take six weeks or it may take six months, but you will be moving toward your goals as you work through *Imagine Loving Your Work.*

What Are Your Expectations?

One of the first exercises clients complete in career counseling is defining what they want to get out of the process. Your goals and expectations will influence how you will use the process we describe. Please take a few moments now to consider, then answer, the following:

The methods shared in *Imagine Loving Your Work* will take both my time and energy.

As I begin, what are my expectations for this investment?

_____

_____

_____

_____

_____

_____

CHAPTER 2

It Wasn't Always
Nine to Five:
The Nature of Work

et's take a trip down memory lane. Actually, we need to travel beyond a time in memory for most of us, back to the days when many folks worked in agriculture.

Looking Back

In past times, women (and men) worked around the home. Most people lived on farms and the livelihood of the family depended on agricultural production. The farm was not only their work, but their means of survival. Work was something that wasn't removed from the family, or separate from day to day living; it was part of everyone's life.

Each day on the farm, family members took care of those things that needed to be done to insure that they would eat and have shelter and clothing. Most of the activities engaged in were directly related to one's ability to survive. Everyone participated in their particular chores, functions, or roles. Men were primarily responsible for planting and harvesting crops and handling the animals. Women did the cooking and cleaning, minded the children and tended things in the house. They sewed and did handiwork, raised vegetable and flower gardens and canned fruits and vegetables for later use. Children helped with the chores.

The Industrial Age

As factories and manufacturing ushered in the Industrial Age, the nature of work changed. Moving away from the family farm, folks started to settle in cities and towns. "Work" became something that was less directly tied to the immediate well-being of the family; in other words, the fruit of one's labor did not end up directly on the dinner table.

As men became involved with work outside of the family, women and children experienced a change in roles, too. There were new opportunities for employment for both women and men in the factories and "sweat shops" in growing American cities. At the beginning of the Industrial era, men were the dominant work force. More men than women were employed in manufacturing because men were seen as the family bread winners. Although women continued to perform their traditional roles with the home and with children, more and more began to take jobs outside of the home as well.

Most of us have heard our parents or grandparents talk about the effects that the Great Depression had on their lives. This devastating period of American history left most of those who found work feeling "lucky" to have a job, any job. Far from being concerned with "career satisfaction," their concern was with survival for themselves and their families.

The War Years

A huge shift in the dynamics of the work force happened during World War II. Suddenly, the male work force was needed for service in the Armed Forces. Manufacturers, pushing hard to meet the demand for military supplies, had to quickly identify and lure a new force into the workplace—the women of America took off kitchen aprons, packed metal lunch boxes, donned coveralls, and went to work for the war effort.

Companies, faced with the special work needs of women and a compelling reason to meet those needs, established on-site day care centers and sponsored recreational programs for their women workers. There were many non-traditional work options for women during this time, including jobs as welders, construction workers, mechanics, and truck drivers.

When the "boys" came home from war, women were sent back home and into their traditional roles. But the workplace, and women, had been influenced forever by the war experience. Some women found it hard to give up their independence and the feelings of competence and achievement gained from working outside of the home. Some women discovered that they liked "being the boss." Some women enjoyed the feeling of independence that having their own money offered.

Despite the good feelings many women had about their work experiences, most bowed to social pressure and returned to home and hearth. Women were expected to give up the jobs that they held in favor of the returning soldiers. In the 1950s, many women who worked outside of the home were looked upon with skepticism. Society valued and rewarded the homemaker and mother more than the "career girl."

The Information Age

As manufacturing and industry moved into the "Information Age," beginning in the 1960s, women again entered the work force in large numbers. Increased production meant that there was a need for more workers, and women were available.

The influence of the women's movement played a role in the increasing number of working women. With broader views of their options, women now demanded the same avenues for self-fulfillment available to men; avenues which included greater access to the workplace and more opportunities for advancement, training, education, and recognition once they are there.

Today, economic inflation has also created the need for families to have two incomes. To afford the spiraling costs of a home, food, clothing, automobiles, and the other necessities and luxuries of modern life, it has become increasingly necessary that both partners work to support the family. As the divorce rate climbs, more women are working to either contribute to, or fully support, their families.

In 1976, there were 8.3 million two-income families. By 1988, this figure had jumped to 13.4 million. As the divorce rate increased, more single parents needed to work to support themselves and their children. In 1960, only 11% of women with children under the age of six worked. In 1987, this percentage had jumped to a whopping 52%. In 1976 only 31% of women reported that they were working (or actively seeking work) within a year of giving birth. In a 1988 survey, this figure had risen to 51%. As a future trend, it is estimated that by the year 2000 nearly two-thirds of the entrants into the work force will be women.

In the United States, one half of all women aged fifteen and over are in the work force. Women make up approximately 45% of the paid work force in our country, and one in seven are "professional" employees. Women are deciding that work is an important part of their lives, for financial as well as personal reasons. Women work to find personal challenge, to express their skills and talents, and to enhance their satisfaction.

Working provides us with information about our value in a broader, societal sense. Our earnings affirm that our abilities have a market value, a validation not afforded to the homemaking aspect of our lives. Further, work provides us feedback about what we do well. It provides us with a mirror in which we can see reflected what sort of people we are.

Looking Forward

Yes, images and roles and traditions continue to change, and they change rapidly! Some of the trends that will influence the workplace of the future will be directly related to responding to the needs of women employees. Job sharing and other alternative work arrangements will be available for working women who want to balance the demands of work and family.

Increased availability of on-site child care and flexibility for care of elderly parents will be incorporated into employee benefit packages. Individuals may coordinate two part-time work assignments in the future, rather than maintain one full-time job, in order to gain schedule flexibility or pursue varying career options and interests.

Current trends indicate that the number of jobs in the future will grow faster than the number of people (especially white males) available to fill them. This means that there will continue to be more employment options available for female and/or minority job seekers. Women will have increasing access to non-traditional career paths as the proportionate number of men entering the work force declines. Women are living longer and having fewer children now than at any time in history. This means that they have more years available to pursue other means of self-expression, including a career.

Women in the Workplace

While men have a long and varied history of work outside the home, women are comparatively recent entrants into the workplace. Most women didn't have the experience of hearing mom and her friends sitting around the kitchen table discussing the best way to negotiate a salary increase at work.

As more and more women enter the work force, increasing opportunities to meet female mentors and role models will exist. This will further enhance women's career opportunities and expand our options. This will also help women gain skill in management and supervision—an area where women's skills have traditionally been criticized.

Actually, women demonstrate different management skills than men do. This is an area relatively new to women: we are a bit "green" as managers in the traditional sense. In the areas of management and supervision, women can benefit from having the support and guidance of a mentor or coach. And this is a role that either women or men can fill for each other.

There is a great deal in current literature about the "female advantage" in management. Increasingly, there is a belief that the "natural" skills and talents women possess lend themselves to effective leadership. Women approach work, and their working relationships, in a manner different from men. More collaborative, more interpersonally supportive, more interested in communicating with their coworkers, women are naturally more in tune with the needs of the modern workplace.

Many businesses striving to compete in a global economy are implementing work strategies that demand a high level of involvement and cooperation from their personnel. In the past, there was a paternal relationship between management and workers on the job site. In jobs that were primarily involved with manufacturing a product, there were different expectations about the role of "worker" and "boss." Workers were primarily concerned with survival and earning a paycheck to keep home and hearth functioning. The boss and company were the benevolent "father," with the influence to hire and fire, the authority to enforce the rules, and the power to dole out the money. In this top-down mode, workers took orders, did their jobs, and went home at the end of the day, probably not too concerned about whether they liked their work or not.

Now the workplace has become even more diverse. There are greater and greater pressures for a change in the outdated paternal work relationship of the past. As the nature of work has changed, as we move toward an information and service-based economy, our views about what work should mean to us have changed also. Concerns about career satisfaction and creating greater happiness are a part of many on-going discussions in today's workplace. In the past, to be a good worker or provider, one went along with and followed the rules. You were expected to do your job, follow the procedures, and neither ask questions nor make waves—often staying in the same job for a long time.

Instead of mere survival and just "getting by," workers today are more concerned about finding meaning in what they do, looking for quality as well as quantity in their life's work. In today's workplace, employees want to know why things are done the way they are and contribute ideas for improvements. Workers now speak up and ask to have their needs met. The workplace has become more dynamic and interactive; it is a place that is undergoing constant change. There are now fewer rules and less structure than in the past. Workers are becoming more like partners in the business, rather than just "worker bees."

"Job security" is often expressed as an important consideration when clients are making career decisions. While influenced by numerous variables, usually this means that the person expects the job they accept to last indefinitely. They want to know that their source of income is protected. Yet today's workplace is constantly changing. This will continue to be the pattern in the future. There is really no such thing as "job security" any more. The market is far too changeable to guarantee any of us an indefinite job.

Women have brought new concerns into the workplace. How does one juggle the demands of children and a career? How does one succeed in the role of supervisor or manager, while still being a woman and using her "feminine" traits? How does one use those natural talents and skills to create more job satisfaction for herself and others? How does one get her needs met while still supporting a family? How does one find, and afford, quality child care?

In the past, women have felt the disadvantage of having few career women as role models for their professional development. We have also faced discrimination and sexual harassment on the job. Our opportunities often have been limited by a lack of either appropriate education or professional mentors to help us learn "the rules of the game" and champion us through the corporate structure. We typically earn less than men who hold the same jobs and there continues to be competition for choice positions.

We have surveyed women about their work beliefs and needs. Read what some of them have shared:

"I expect to have a balanced life. My husband and family come first, but I'm not willing to have a job just for money and time away from home. I still want a creative outlet just to express me."

"I wish I could always (or almost always) enjoy my work. Since

two-thirds of my time is spent on the job (not counting sleep), I want to have a happy, satisfying career."

"(My career) is who I am...it's very important to me! (It) gives me a sense of pride (to) have people respect me for what I do."

"I want my career to fulfill my life away from home. It's my second life. I'd like harmony between the two."

"I want my work to be an integral part of my life. I want to be rewarded financially and with personal satisfaction."

"I want to have a vision again, instead I'm just working."

The nature of work has changed a great deal since our grandparents, or even our parents, were young. Technological advances, economic pressures, changing societal norms, and shifting demographics have all influenced dynamic and exciting changes in the workplace.

How will you respond to these changes? The answer to this question is contained in what you believe about work. The next chapter will help you explore these beliefs.

CHAPTER 3

Everybody's Gotta Believe in Something: Your Personal Work Heritage

Your work beliefs are the ideas you have about what work is, what it means in your life, and what you expect your career to be like. Your beliefs result from your observations and experiences throughout life, not only from your own time on the job, but from the time your parents and grandparents spent working, too.

By looking at our work heritage (the rich texture of information we received about work from our families and our culture), we develop an increased awareness of our own beliefs about work. When we know what our beliefs are and where they came from, we are able to make better, more conscious decisions for the future.

Understanding and accepting our work heritage helps us make sense out of the decisions and choices we have made that brought us to the place we are today. We can examine our beliefs and decide which of them we want to keep and which we want to change. We can choose options now and in the future that create greater work satisfaction.

Garbage In, Garbage Out

You may be familiar with a phrase often used in the computer world: "Garbage In, Garbage Out." It means that the quality of the product we get at the end of any process will only be as good as the materials and work that went into its creation. This is also true for our beliefs and how they influence our career decision making process.

Operating unconsciously from your work belief heritage can be a form of "garbage in." The result will often be career decisions that do not fit your needs, talents, values, or wants. It is impossible for us to make good decisions about our work choices—to make choices that satisfy us—if we have not yet clarified what kinds of beliefs form the framework of those decisions. We need to examine where our beliefs came from in order to understand how they were formed and why they took the shape that they did. Knowing this, we can consciously decide what to keep, what may work for us in the future, and what is outdated or inappropriate for us at this time in our lives.

Adopting and carrying on the beliefs of our parents or other family members can cause us to expect either too much or too little from ourselves and our work.

It Has to Fit You

When you examine the work beliefs your parents and grandparents held, it may be apparent to you that what they believed about the nature of work was appropriate for their experience and time in history. It may also be apparent that these beliefs are now outdated, or sexist, or simply not right for you. What was appropriate and customary for your grandfather in 1930 is unlikely to work for you, as a woman, in the 1990s.

Sometimes people express a desire to return to "simpler times," but the truth is that each time in history has had its own trials and triumphs. With an understanding of our work heritage, including the options and choices we saw modeled for women, we can move toward the future with a new ability to create and implement solutions that better meet our hopes, dreams, and aspirations.

Influencing Your Beliefs

Pamela was within five years of retirement when she decided to seek out a career counselor. She felt burned-out in her job. Early retirement seemed like a way to explore other work options and perhaps find her passion. She felt terrified of becoming a "bag lady" after she retired, and her fear was getting in her way as she attempted to make plans for leaving work and moving on with her life.

She thought a great deal about her life and work before starting career counseling, but was unable to find a reason for her panic over retirement. As she said, "Babies are not born afraid of being a bag lady. What happened?"

As Pamela considered her family's work beliefs, she made an amazing discovery. She traced a fear of poverty through seven generations of her family. She recalled hearing her own parents' dinner conversations and their fears about meeting their financial needs for retirement. Her father complained about his work. Her mother hated her job. Somewhere in the discussion, Pamela always heard them say, "Well, there are only a few more years until we can retire. Then we will get to do what we want to do, if we have the money." Suddenly, her concerns about retirement made perfect sense.

Armed with this insight, she made conscious decisions about how to arrange her finances so that she felt secure about the future and safe about leaving her job. One year later, she retired.

Tracing Your Family Tree

Now it is time to take a look at the work heritage you inherited from your family. What did you learn that helps or hinders you in making satisfying career decisions for yourself, now and in the future?

Perhaps you never met your grandparents, or one of your parents was absent for a part of your childhood. You still know valuable information about this person, or persons, however, by what you heard from other family members, your parents, and friends. Just as you "inherited" beliefs from your parents, so too did they inherit beliefs from their parents.

For example, perhaps you didn't know your grandfather. But you heard that he ran a dairy farm; that he abandoned the family when your father was young; and that he lived in the midwest during the Dust Bowl years. Let's say that you have a picture of him standing beside his team of work horses.

You now have the beginnings of an image of this person. Try to paint a picture of your "missing person" by creatively piecing together the information you do know about them with the things you imagine about him or her. If you were an author, how would you develop this character in your story?

_____

_____

_____

_____

_____

_____

_____

_____

_____

_____

_____

Using this diagram of your family, fill in the names of your parents and grandparents.

Genograms

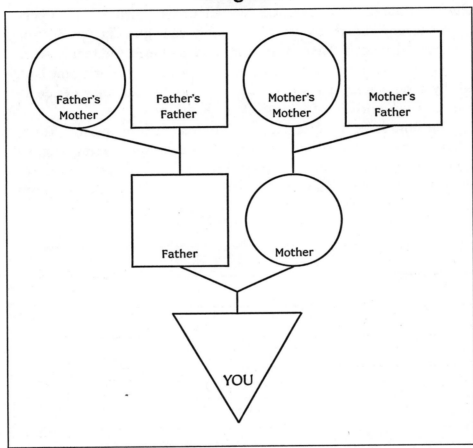

On the following pages are a series of statements for you to answer as though you were speaking for these members of your family. Your answers to the following questions need not be factually correct or accurate. Answer them as closely as you can in the way you think your family member would, but if necessary, allow yourself to be creative and "fill in the blanks."

Father's Father   Name: _____

For your Father's Father (your paternal grandfather), respond to the following statements:

Work is ... _____

_____

_____

_____

Money is ... _____

_____

_____

_____

Success is ... _____

_____

_____

_____

To be a good person ... _____

_____

_____

_____

My advice to you about work is ... _____

_____

_____

_____

Father's Mother   Name: _____

For your Father's Mother (your paternal grandmother), respond to each of the following:

Work is ... _____

_____

_____

_____

Money is ... _____

_____

_____

_____

Success is ... _____

_____

_____

_____

To be a good person ... _____

_____

_____

_____

My advice to you about work is ... _____

_____

_____

_____

Mother's Father   Name: _____

For your Mother's Father (your maternal grandfather), respond to each of the following:

Work is … _____

_____

_____

_____

Money is … _____

_____

_____

_____

Success is … _____

_____

_____

_____

To be a good person … _____

_____

_____

_____

My advice to you about work is … _____

_____

_____

_____

Mother's Mother   Name: _____

As your Mother's Mother (your maternal grandmother), respond to the following statements:

Work is ... _____

_____

_____

_____

Money is ... _____

_____

_____

_____

Success is ... _____

_____

_____

_____

To be a good person ... _____

_____

_____

_____

My advice to you about work is ... _____

_____

_____

_____

Father   Name: _____

If your Father were speaking, how would he respond to the following?

Work is ... _____

_____

_____

_____

Money is ... _____

_____

_____

_____

Success is ... _____

_____

_____

_____

To be a good person ... _____

_____

_____

_____

My advice to you about work is ... _____

_____

_____

_____

Mother   Name: _____

Consider how your Mother would respond to the following:

Work is ... _____

_____

_____

_____

Money is ... _____

_____

_____

_____

Success is ... _____

_____

_____

_____

To be a good person ... _____

_____

_____

_____

My advice to you about work is ... _____

_____

_____

_____

Significant Person   Name: _____

Their relationship to you:_____

Were there other significant adults in your life? If so, respond to the following as though they were talking to you:

Work is ... _____

_____

_____

_____

Money is ... _____

_____

_____

_____

Success is ... _____

_____

_____

_____

To be a good person ... _____

_____

_____

_____

My advice to you about work is ... _____

_____

_____

_____

List what clues you now have about yourself from this exercise.

For example: One client discovered as a result of her answers that her family believed it was best to own their own businesses, rather than work for someone else. This was a clue for her about why she found working for a "boss" to be stressful.

_____

_____

_____

_____

_____

What are your own beliefs about work? Who influenced these beliefs?

Belief   Who Influenced

_____   _____

_____   _____

_____   _____

_____   _____

_____   _____

_____   _____

_____   _____

Which beliefs work well and are ones you want to keep? Which beliefs would you like to change?

_____

_____

_____

_____

_____

_____

What new beliefs would you like to have?

_____

_____

_____

_____

What similarities do you see between your family's beliefs and yours? For example, your family believes that "work is hard." Have you carried out this belief in your life by choosing to do work that you find physically and/or mentally taxing?

_____

_____

_____

_____

Values, beliefs, and the truths that we learned from family form the foundation of our lives. When we start examining these core areas of our lives it can feel like we are walking on shaky ground. We may feel uncertain, unclear, or unstable and it can be frightening to consider change in these areas of our lives that seem so central to who we are.

It can also be a freeing experience. There is no satisfaction in living your life by other's beliefs. It doesn't matter who those beliefs come from: if they are not the ones you hold dear, they will not ring true in your life. Knowing where some of your ideas come from—the source of your belief system—can provide you with renewed energy and freedom to make changes. It provides an explanation for some of the decisions and choices you may have made in the past. This knowledge will allow you to make different decisions or choices in the future, if you desire. Career satisfaction is based on honoring who you are and what you believe to be true.

Fear

As we move toward adulthood, we leave behind our fear of ghosts and goblins, ferocious tigers in the bedroom closet, or the playground bully. Sometimes, as we get bigger, we think we have conquered fear and that we will not be confronted by new fears (or old ones) as we face our day-to-day life.

In reality, there are things in adulthood that are frightening, too. Fear of failure. Fear of the unknown. Fear of being hurt. Our feelings of fear are real, whether we think they are rational or not. It is important to acknowledge when something we are facing, be it a career change or an interview, causes us to feel afraid.

Admitting that things are frightening or scary is the first step in resolving the fear so that we can move on. Facing our fears, and continuing to move forward toward our goals, is part of the step-by-step process for making a positive career change.

As you explore the exercises in this guide, and as you make new discoveries about your career choices, you will probably confront some feelings of fear. Use this space to start a list of those tasks, thoughts, or issues which you feel afraid or scared about. Keep adding to the list as other fears or anxieties surface.

Fears List

_____	_____
_____	_____
_____	_____
_____	_____
_____	_____
_____	_____

When you get your fears down on paper they become more tangible and less intimidating. When you read them, you have a better chance of finding ways to resolve and remove these fears as barriers to your ultimate career satisfaction.

If your fears seem vague or unclear, try answering some of the following questions:

I'm afraid I will/I will not ... _____

_____

I'm afraid someone ... _____

_____

I'm afraid that ... _____

_____

It seems scary to ... _____

_____

I'm afraid to ... _____

_____

I'm afraid of ... _____

_____

A number of years ago, a special person came into the lives of the men and women you wrote about in this chapter—YOU! There were happy smiles and pictures taken. There were little clothes and tiny shoes to try on. There were changes in the family schedule.

And everyone wondered what you would be like as you grew up.

CHAPTER 4

The Child in Your Past: What Are Little Girls Made Of?

We mentioned in Chapter 1 that clues to what may be missing in your career can be found by reconnecting with your fun, child-like self. Exploring and spending time with the child within you not only can be fun, but also can provide useful information about your natural talents and abilities, likes and interests. Expressing these natural inclinations to their fullest in your work can then create greater job satisfaction.

Meeting the Child Within

For the purpose of our discussion, when we talk about the inner child, we are referring to the part of ourselves that is most like a youngster—enthusiastic and "lit up," rather than the restrained adult. Our inner child is the part of us that responds like a child would to a suggestion or event in our lives—it is the part that is energized by new opportunities and sees life as exciting. That inner child is who we were before we started conforming to peer and adult pressure, before we became "mature adults."

Sometimes, as adults, it is hard to connect with our inner child. If you are not sure if you still have an inner child, think of a recent time when you saw a puppy or a kitten and wanted to take it home, before the adult part thought of a thousand reasons why you "couldn't possibly have a pet right now!" Our inner child speaks to us through the things we would love to do, if only we had the courage or were not afraid of what other people might think.

When you ask a group of first graders what they like to do, their hands shoot up into the air. Some of them even raise two hands, they're so anxious to share what brings them joy. They don't need to spend much time thinking about what they like, they just know. There is a direct connection between their likes and their willingness to tell you about them. They don't worry about what someone else thinks about their choices, or whether or not their answers are "stupid." They know what they like and they tell you.

As we grow older, we tend to get more concerned about "what others will think" and about "how we look" if we do the fun things our inner child loves to do. As adults, when we ask ourselves what we like, there is often a delayed reaction. Sometimes there is no voice, no answer. That is why we need to re-connect and spend time with our inner child. It is important to feel again what it is like to be the kid you were, to have contact with what pleased you, to know what you really liked to do.

Carla created greater career satisfaction when she honored her inner child. In college, Carla majored in horticulture. She loved plants and growing things. But ten years later Carla found herself working graveyard shift as a supervisor in a dark, sterile factory. While the job paid well and had good benefits, she felt like she was withering up and dying a slow death there.

Then, Carla purchased an acre of land as an investment with money she saved from her supervisor salary. And when she began career counseling, she soon reconnected with her passion for plants and growing things and decided that what she really wanted to do was open a nursery. She took classes on how to run her own business and made plans to realize her hopes and dreams. On her birthday, Carla quit her job at the factory and launched her nursery business. While she agrees that it is hard to start a new business, she also says that she has never been happier in her life.

It Isn't Always Easy

Carla confronted one of the truths about following one's dreams—it isn't always easy. Discovering and following your desires by reconnecting with the child within involves taking risks, stretching yourself to the maximum, doing things that you have never done before, and letting go of your old, comfortable ways.

This may involve giving up some of your feelings of security, either emotional or financial, in order to realize your goals. For example, let's explore parenting. Most of us believe that choosing to rear children is a worthwhile goal. But when the bills pile up or when sick kids keep us up all night, we realize that choosing to parent is not an easy goal to embrace.

Doing something of importance puts us on the line and makes us vulnerable. Think of an artist preparing for a gallery show—wishing to share her creations, but afraid of what people will think of her work. Our dreams, like art work, are so personal that we often feel vulnerable when sharing them. Only you can decide how important your dreams are and how much you are willing to risk to make them come true.

As you learn more about yourself through the exercises in this guide, and as you create ideas about possible new careers, you will then develop a better understanding of what you are and are not willing to do to make your dreams come true. Remember, you needn't take all of the steps to a new career in one week, one month, or even one year. You can decide when and what steps you want to implement: you are in control of your journey.

Our Role Models

Our mothers, and the other women in our families and in our lives were important role models as we were growing and maturing. In your life, did these women work outside of the home? What kinds of things did you hear them discuss? What did you hear them say about their roles as wives, mothers, workers, friends? Were there implied notions or assumptions in your family, spoken or unspoken, that you would become a wife and mother or enter a particular kind of career? Were you expected to go to college?

We believe that most parents want to help their children be happy. Sometimes they will say to a son or daughter, "You can do anything you want to do." Well, alright, but what is "anything?" How can a child know what their options are? Perhaps mom and dad felt pressured as children to become something they did not want to be, or maybe they just did not know how one goes about identifying and then getting what one wants.

Some parents want to help, but have few clues about how to identify and choose careers. "You can do anything you want to do," while said with the best of intentions, fails to provide helpful guidance and critical direction for learning what making a career choice is all about. Children who hear that they can "be anything" are often left wondering what it is they want. They didn't get solid support or learn ways to discover what they were good at, what they liked, and what they could do.

Messages from Outside the Family

Television and the media have played a large role in influencing the career and life choices of children. For example, when Marti was little, she dreamed of being Davy Crockett. She and her dad used to watch the Davy Crockett show on television. She remembers that they pretended to shoot the "bad guys" together. Vicki and her neighbor, Marina, on the other hand, pretended that they were folk singers, like Marianne Faithful and Joan Baez. They would imagine themselves appearing on The Ed Sullivan Show.

If you watched television when you were growing up, you probably saw the women on "Leave It To Beaver," "Bewitched," "I Dream of Jeannie," "I Love Lucy," and the like. Now, take a moment to consider what you did and did not see these women doing on television. What influence do you think these subtle and not so subtle messages had on you as you made your career plans? Who did you imagine yourself imitating?

Perhaps you got the message when you were a little girl that Prince Charming would someday come into your life. You also learned that you should always look your best (after all, you didn't know when he would show up), that you should be nice, and that you should mind your manners. Then, when a potential prince finally appears, you mustn't be too smart nor beat him at games (after all, Prince Charming has a fragile ego which you probably learned that you are also responsible for). Little girls receive many overt and covert messages from society about how the game of life is played. These messages often get translated into adult realities that, in turn, affect the decisions we make about our careers and our lives. When carried into adulthood, and the work world, these messages affect our career choices as well as how we interact with men and other women in the workplace.

Some of the women we have talked with are actually angry at having to go to work. The message they heard as little girls was not only that Prince Charming would come along, but that he would also take care of them for a lifetime. They would stay home and rear the children as their part of the "deal." Later, as adults, often through death or divorce, these women are faced with a role they never anticipated—that of entering the work force in order to support themselves and their children.

Other women entered the work force willingly, but never expected to stay there for very long. For one reason or another, however, Prince Charming never came along. Women in this category may be angry because they chose to postpone or limit their pursuit of a career in anticipation of a prince taking care of them. One day she discovers that she is responsible for all that happens in her life, and she feels unprepared. She may not have learned how to fix the car, repair things around the house, invest money, or handle other problems that she thought would never surface for her.

Some women choose a career, regardless of whether or not they marry, and pursue it to the best of their abilities. For these women, there are often other frustrations. Acknowledging the messages you heard as a child, and honoring the anger or other feelings you have about working as an adult, are important ingredients in the process of choosing a career.

Keeping Your Balance

Remember, too, that to one extent or another, we all have some unpleasant memories of events that happened to us as children. We confronted the bully on the playground, someone shouted words that hurt our feelings, we fell down and broke an arm, we failed to win first place with our science project, our third grade teacher "hated" us, and so forth. Please keep in mind, however, that our focus in this career guide is on the positive, fun memories you have of yourself as a kid.

We believe there are few, if any, clues about career satisfaction in the negative messages received from the adults in your life who said you could not, or would not, amount to anything. If you were around "toxic" adults (parents, teachers, relatives, or other significant adults), the negative input from them is what you want to let go of and not use as you make career decisions.

Their input was based on their own poor self-concepts and negative experiences. You may have been told you were lazy, stupid, fat, or ugly just because they were having a bad day. Or perhaps they wanted to limit you as a child; perhaps you were sent to your room or ordered to sit down and be quiet. One client remembered being told by her kindergarten teacher that she was "the dumbest student" the teacher had ever had in class.

As children, we didn't know that a truly appropriate response to this kindergarten teacher might have been, "Oh, Ms. Jones, I see that you are obviously having a bad day and I will ignore that last comment." Children can't differentiate between accurate and inaccurate input from adults. Like little sponges, we take it all in, and in our own child-like mind, try to make sense of it. Some of our conclusions about ourselves from these statements are erroneous, but we continue to hold on to them long after childhood.

Sometimes, when we focus on these negative aspects of our child-hood, we concentrate only on how they hurt us or made us feel bad. We forget some of the good that can come from even our most negative experiences. For every adversity in our lives, we have created ways to cope and make the best of the situation. In truth, you can come to appreciate the value and marketability of the positive skills you learned from coping with dysfunctional situations.

Turning it Around

Laura's father was alcoholic. Every day when she came home from school, she had to be prepared to deal with this situation. She never knew if her father would come home sober, or drunk, or if he would even come home at all. Laura didn't know if there would be a fight, or if she should just head straight to her room, or if things would be calm that day. No child should have to deal with this situation, but Laura gained a valuable skill as she learned to cope with her father's alcoholism.

For one thing, she learned to walk into a room or into a group and quickly size up or evaluate the overall mood. Now, she can go into a meeting and sense if there is tension or conflict. Laura doesn't have to think about this, she just knows what is going on after her years of practice at home. This is a highly marketable skill. It helps Laura work more effectively with committees, groups, and boards.

It is important to reclaim and acknowledge these kinds of skills, regardless of their source. In looking at career satisfaction, we want to look at the pieces we have inside ourselves. All of us have aspects that we are blind to. We have an inaccurate picture of ourselves because of our growing up experience, or because people around us gave us wrong information about who we were, or because we didn't think that this, or that, was important.

The Kid Connections chapter that follows contains exercises and suggestions to help you make contact with your inner child, the kid-like part deep inside. Doing the exercises will help you gain insight and remember what you used to be like (and still could be like) without the "mature and responsible" adult getting in the way.

Now, get your crayons out. Put your favorite old records on the stereo. Pull out scrapbooks, pictures, or other mementos of yourself as a child. Then turn to the Kid Connections chapter and have fun!

CHAPTER 5

Kid Connections:
Getting in Touch
With the Child Within

M ost of us, as we grow older, give up the things of childhood and take on an "adult" persona. Sometimes it is hard to remember things about ourselves as children, so getting in touch with that natural child inside of us might take some concentrated effort. Yet, our natural child knows a wealth of information about what we do well, what we enjoy, and what comes easily to us in work or play. Reconnecting with this aspect of ourselves is vital in choosing career options that offer satisfaction.

This chapter is filled with a number of creative suggestions for spending time with your "kid." You can play, reminisce, eat, watch television, rent your favorite movie, and brag about the crazy things (and the wonderful things) you did when you were younger.

Pick one exercise, or do them all! The main objective is to have fun while unlocking your childhood memories. Remember—these exercises are just suggestions—you can choose to complete as many of them as you desire. And for even more fun, make up some Kid Connections of your own!

Getting Started

First, we believe it helps to have some of the "things" from your child-hood around when you want to get back in touch with the kid that you were. So...

➤ Use your family photo album. Go through the pictures of you, your parents, your siblings, your friends, and relatives. Spend time with each picture and remember what you can about the day it was taken and what you were doing at the time.

➤ Draw a picture of your room, your house, your neighborhood, or your classroom. Or, draw another location that was impor-tant to you. (See "Childhood" section in Chapter 15.)

➤ If you have kept them, look over your report cards from school. Report cards are an excellent source of information. In the com-ments section, you can often find examples of your natural tal-ents, behaviors, and inclinations. Pay close attention to the positive comments your teachers made about your unique tal-ents and skills.

➤ Revisit projects, drawings, or art work that you completed in school that you or your family have saved.

➤ Think about your favorite games, stories, or toys. Perhaps you can remember television shows or movies you liked, or how you liked to spend your time.

➤ Ask friends and associates who are about the same age as you are what kinds of memories they have of things that were pop-ular during the years you were growing up.

➤ Talk with your parents, siblings, or relatives and ask them to tell you about yourself as a child. Or, think about the stories you have heard other members of your family tell about you.

Telling Your Story

Think of your childhood years as a timeline of events. Place marks for each of your birthdays between one and eighteen on a line. Then, go back over your childhood and add marks for the important events you remember. These events could be times that were especially fun or memorable (perhaps when you attained special achievements, honors, successes); times that were turning points in your life; times that were milestones and have influenced how you live your life today.

   These events can be things that you did by yourself or with others. They can be big things or little, pleasant or unpleasant. If you get stuck, ask yourself the following question: "I'm _____ years old. (Fill in a year that is hard for you to remember.) What am I doing?"

Birth   Age 9

Age 9   Age 18

Think carefully about your childhood. Which events seem to be the most important to you? What kinds of events did you choose to put on your timeline? Why? What does this tell you about your kid?

_____

_____

_____

_____

_____

_____

_____

_____

_____

_____

_____

Too Much

Adults often tell children that they are "too much" of something or other, usually in those moments when the child manages to frustrate the adult in some way.

Here is a list of examples of things you may have heard you were too much of:

Bossy   Starry-eyed   Tomboy

Talkative   Boisterous   Intense   Social

Disruptive   Emotional   Loud

Rough   Trusting   Quiet   Smart

Friendly   Bashful   Flirty

Assertive   Exuberant   Sensitive   Inquisitive

Busy   Slow   Messy   Shy

Chatty   Aggressive   Naive   Noisy

Ignoring damaging or hurtful comments, notice clues about your natural self in what you were told you were "too much" of as a child. Write your list here:

_____   _____

_____   _____

_____   _____

_____   _____

Negative messages you may have heard, such as "too lazy," "too dumb," or "too fat," tell you nothing useful about yourself. (Yes, most of us were lazy about the things we disliked doing, like chores. However, we were up and raring to go for those things we liked doing! Those negative, hurtful comments were made by insensitive adults.) If you have any of these three on your list, or other comments you remember that were especially hurtful or insulting, cross them off now.

What kinds of clues do these phrases provide us? For example, were you "too talkative" as a child? You were probably told this when your desire to talk interfered with something that a parent, teacher, or other adult wanted you to do. It may have even shown up on your report card. The potential career clue in this message is that you are naturally gifted with the ability and desire to talk to other people. If you naturally enjoy talking to others, this is a talent that you can use easily, comfortably, and successfully as a part of your career. People who were talkative as children often enjoy success as adults when they go into professions that take advantage of this talent. They can have careers as public speakers, teachers, actors, salespeople, customer service representatives, tour guides, lawyers, or politicians. They can get paid for being talkative.

What if you were told that you were "too slow" as a child? Children who take their time on projects and school assignments are often concerned with getting everything done correctly. They like to take time because they want to make sure they have followed all of the steps and attended to all of the details. As adults, these people do well in careers that take advantage of their natural attention to detail, and to a concern for precision and correctness. They might be happy in careers as accountants, statisticians, editors, doctors, secretaries, claims processors, or tax preparers, among others.

Carefully consider the "too much" statements that you heard about yourself as a child. What do they tell you about your natural gifts or ways of being? Do these statements help you understand more about yourself today?

_____

_____

_____

_____

Which of these natural gifts are not being used well enough in your work?

_____   _____

_____   _____

What does this tell you about your inner child?

_____

_____

_____

_____

_____

_____

"I Wanna Be A ..."

"What do you want to be when you grow up?" seems to be one of the most common questions that children get asked. Our answers were probably never the same twice. When you were asked this question as a kid, what did you say? You probably changed your mind as you were growing up, too, as you learned about more career options from school, television, reading, or other sources.

If you have forgotten what you used to tell folks when they asked, perhaps you can remember what you liked to pretend to be. What kinds of people or characters did you fantasize about or play the part of in games? What kinds of things did you find fascinating? Were there particular kinds of people that you liked to read about? What were your hobbies?

Read through this list carefully. Circle all of the people/things/occupations you remember pretending about when you were a child. Add others that you think of at the end of the list.

Cowboy	Ballerina	Horse	Doctor
Police	Writer	Movie Star	Indian
Someone Important		Firefighter	President
Mommy	Artist	Fashion Designer	Princess
Soldier	Farmer	Truck Driver	Teacher
Dog	Dancer	Pilot Boss	King
Cat	Singer	Someone Rich	Lawyer
Dentist	Super Hero	Reporter	Snow White

_____ _____ _____ _____

Now spend some time thinking about your selections. What clues about yourself can you find in the kinds of things you liked to pretend to be as a child? Obvious reasons for your selections will probably come easily to mind as you consider each one.

Look also for the less-than-obvious reasons for your selections. For example, let's say that one of your selections was Snow White. What kinds of clues are there in wanting to be Snow White? Perhaps it was because you thought that she got to wear pretty clothes. Maybe it was because a handsome prince came along and rescued her. One of the less obvious clues, however, may be that Snow White appealed to you because she had seven guys to boss around! Look at your selections again for the less obvious clues. What might they be?

_____

_____

_____

_____

_____

_____

_____

Going for the Gold...

On this page, write a story about your personal best. It can be your proudest moment. It can be an example of your most outrageous behavior. It can be the time you got in the most trouble. It can be when you were the happiest. Write a story about one of the outstanding memories of your childhood.

My Personal Best

by _____

_____

_____

_____

_____

_____

_____

_____

_____

_____

_____

_____

_____

_____

_____

_____

_____

_____

_____

How would you describe the child who did what you just wrote about? Is she active, curious, creative, motivated, organized, happy? What does this story tell you about yourself?

_____

_____

_____

_____

Time to Color!

Draw a picture of yourself, doing something that you liked to do when you were a child (under the age of twelve). Choose a memory of a happy time. As you think about those times, draw what first comes to mind. It is important to just go ahead and sketch, and not be critical or judgmental of yourself or your artistic skill. It does not have to be a perfect drawing. Use stick figures and crayons, if you have them.

Now, take a close look at your picture. Absorb the image for a moment, then close your eyes. Imagine yourself in the drawing you just made, once again engaged in the favorite pastime or involved in the actions you have drawn. Imagine taking part in the scene, and let it unfold in your mind. As you imagine yourself once again in this picture, look around. What do you see? Who are the people in the picture with you? What are you doing? What can you smell? What can you reach out and touch? What do you hear? Allow yourself to fully experience all aspects of this activity.

When you have completed this visualization, use the following lines to write a story about your picture. Explain what is happening in the drawing and how you feel as the kid in the picture.

_____

_____

_____

_____

_____

From the picture and story, what additional clues do you now have about your inner child?

_____

_____

_____

_____

How Did You Earn Money as a Kid?

How did you make or get money when you were younger?

Selling magazine subscriptions   Whining/Pleading/Begging

From the Tooth Fairy   Washing the car

Returning bottles   Paper route

Baby-sitting   Lemonade stand

From your allowance   Taking care of animals

Mowing lawns

How old were you when you earned money for the first time?_____

What was your favorite part of this job (or several jobs)?

_____

_____

_____

_____

_____

_____

_____

_____

_____

_____

What did you do with the money that you earned? Did you save some of it, spend all of it? What did you buy?

_____

_____

_____

_____

_____

_____

_____

What was one of your greatest successes in this venture?

_____

_____

_____

_____

_____

_____

_____

_____

What does this tell you about your natural child?

_____

_____

_____

_____

_____

_____

Here are some examples of women who showed an entrepreneurial spirit at a young age:

Barb was thirteen when she got her first baby-sitting job with a neighbor family. It didn't take her long to discover that there wasn't much about watching young children that she enjoyed, but she didn't have too many other alternatives for earning spending money.

As she considered what she could do to make her work more interesting, she decided to take her camera along when she went to baby-sit. Barb loved to take photographs, and the children liked to ham it up for the camera. After she got her photos developed, Barb arranged them in creative collages. She shared one of her collages with her "charges'" parents, and they offered to buy it from her. They showed it to their friends, and Barb started getting calls from other families wanting her to photograph their children and create the imaginative collages for them.

Sylvia, on the other hand, loved to help her mother garden. One spring, her mother helped her select and plant a variety of decorative gourds in her own corner of the family's vegetable garden. As the days moved through summer to fall, Sylvia's crop became ready for harvest. She plucked the assorted gourds and loaded them into her wagon.

Making her rounds of neighbors and friends, Sylvia offered her crop for sale. Lower prices for small gourds, higher prices for large ones and pumpkins. Ever the entrepreneur, Sylvia even sold gourds to her mother—but at a discount for her help in tending the plants.

Lastly, Krista was the oldest of five children. She learned early how to organize and command her siblings, and she developed a system for turning this into a profit. First, she polled neighbors and family friends and developed jobs to do, such as walking the dog, mowing the yard, or washing the windows. After she had developed ten assignments or so, she organized her brothers and sisters into a work force, assigned them to specific jobs, and sent them out to accomplish the tasks. When they returned home, Krista would go to the neighbor and collect payment for the job. She'd take a percentage for herself, subtract expenses, and pay her siblings "wages."

After School

What did you do after school?

Girl Scouts   Camp Fire Girls   Bluebirds

Movies   Brownies

Clubs   Swim   Homework   Chores

Play with a pet   Dance lessons

Gymnastics   4-H   Music lessons

Play at a friend's house   Team sports

_____   _____   _____

Write about your favorite after-school activity. Why was it your favorite?

_____

_____

_____

_____

Did you ever receive special recognition for your activities? If so, what?

_____

_____

_____

_____

Summary: Kid Connections

What clues did you discover about yourself from your "kid" experiences?

_____

_____

_____

_____

What is your natural child-self like? Describe her.

_____

_____

_____

_____

What kinds of things does your natural child like to do? Not do?

_____

_____

_____

_____

What are the clues for your career satisfaction that you observed in your natural child?

_____

_____

_____

_____

Your natural talents and gifts make you unique in the world, different from anyone else. Using these in your work creates satisfaction because it is easier to succeed when you are doing what you do best. Through these exercises, what five qualities, patterns, styles, talents, or gifts did you notice about your natural child that could be honored by or expressed through your work?

_____

_____

_____

_____

_____

What aspects of your natural child need to be better integrated into your work?

_____

_____

_____

_____

You've now had many opportunities to enjoy remembering and spending time with the great kid inside you. You have a new picture of what she is like, what she enjoys, and what makes her special. Seeing her in your mind brings a smile to your face.

This positive, joyful, enthusiastic, playful girl that you were (and who still exists within you) can bring passion and commitment back to your career. She can also help you identify where the fun is in the work you do so that you can develop ways to increase your pleasure in performing your job. By allowing your natural child to fully express herself at work, you can dramatically increase your career satisfaction.

In the next chapter, we will look at and explore your adult picture of yourself.

CHAPTER 6

Creating
An Accurate Picture:
Mirror, Mirror,
Who Am I?

Did you ever go through the Fun House at an amusement park when you were a kid? There were false doors, chutes, and puffs of compressed air to surprise you as you walked through the dark passages. Usually, somewhere within the maze of rooms and corridors, there was a wall of mirrors, distorted with twists and bends in the glass.

The reflection of yourself in these mirrors was wildly different than your real appearance. Some made you look exceptionally tall, others very short. Some made you bend or curve in the middle, others made you appear completely out of proportion. Whatever the mirror's unique feature, the image of yourself reflected in the glass had little resemblance to the way you really looked.

Sometimes, getting to adulthood is like making that journey through the Fun House. Along the way we encounter surprises and events that we never imagined would happen to us. There are false starts, setbacks, and unexpected twists and turns to life. And just like the reflection in the distorted mirror, the image we develop of ourselves does not necessarily reflect who we truly are.

Think back to the exercises you did in earlier chapters. Think about your work heritage. With all the input we have influencing us, all our lives, it may be difficult to form and maintain a totally accurate picture of ourselves.

We all tend to believe things about ourselves that are untrue. By bits and pieces, people's comments, criticism, and stares influence what and who we think we are. These things all attach themselves to us like layers of "cooties" and contribute to a misleading and distorted picture of ourselves.

Finding out what is accurate about yourself now, in the present, is vital to making satisfying career choices and changes. It is time to strip off the layers of "cooties," the erroneous conceptions of yourself. You need to find and fit together the true and undistorted pieces of yourself, combining your natural skills and talents with the abilities you have developed along the way. It is time to make an accurate appraisal of yourself.

Modesty

Women in our culture tend to be raised to be modest, reserved, humble or unpretentious, and to work hard at pleasing and getting along with others. If we failed to behave in this manner, there were some pretty uncomfortable descriptions used for our behavior. We were labeled "vain," "conceited," "self centered," or a "braggart." Perhaps you were "too big for your britches" or "liked to hear yourself talk." Heaven forbid that you would get a "swelled head" or "think too much of yourself."

Jennifer James, Ph.D., author of "Women and the Blues," talks about an important election for student body office in high school. She lost. But only by two votes—hers and that of the other candidate. She lost because "good girls" never vote for themselves. At least, that is what she had been taught.

When Marti was a little girl, she was very cute. Family and friends would often say to her, "Oh, Martha, you're so cute!" Marti's mother believed, however, that Marti would be "hard to handle" as a teenager if she "thought too much of herself." So when comments about her cuteness were made, her mother taught Marti to reply, "No, I'm clean." Apparently, cleanliness was a more modest and acceptable trait for a girl than being cute! This childhood input has influenced Marti's view of herself as an adult.

61

For the next exercise, get your kitchen timer. Using the spaces below, make a list of the talents, skills, qualities, and abilities you bring to an employer. Set your timer for three minutes and see how many you can list in that time.

_____ _____ _____

_____ _____ _____

_____ _____ _____

_____ _____ _____

_____ _____ _____

_____ _____ _____

_____ _____ _____

_____ _____ _____

How many surfaced? Ten? Twenty? Three? The number that you wrote down is a measure of how you are doing with the concept of "modesty." Now, use the next page to make a list of at least fifty (yes, we mean five-zero) skills, talents, qualities, and abilities you have. Give some thought to compliments you have received in the past for things that you have done well. Also, look at performance evaluations, job descriptions, and letters of recommendation. Hint: If you have trouble coming up with all of them on your own, ask your friends or your coworkers for ideas and input. One client asked a friend to accompany her to a park to talk about and share what they appreciated and admired in each other.

In Other People's Eyes

It's true that others often have a more accurate picture of us than we ourselves do because we know all of our own thoughts and feelings, both positive and negative. We know about the times when we were not "nice," when we didn't do just what we were "supposed" to do. We know there were times when we told "little white lies," even though we had been taught that lying was wrong. When we receive a compliment for a "job well done," we think to ourselves that we could have done better.

Listen to those who are not as intimate with your foibles as you: they have valuable information to share about your skills, talents, qualities, and abilities. And don't look for ways to discount their compliments; rather, give yourself permission to accept this valuable input and add it to your list of fifty!

You truly do have a multitude of skills, talents, qualities, and abilities that are outstanding and make you a unique individual. There will be times when you are less patient, less kind, less creative, less honest, less energetic, less detailed, and so forth, than you would like to be: we call this "being human!"

Taking Our Talents for Granted

Often, when we are asked to describe our jobs, we respond with only one or two of the things that we accomplished that day. We often forget to recall all the skills that we must use and possess in order to complete our work. It is as though we have strapped on blinders which keep us from seeing everything clearly and fully.

One helpful way to get a better idea of all that you do on the job is to keep a job log. Before lunch or during a break, take a moment to write down what you have been doing with your time. Keep this log for a two week period, as you have the time. At the end of two weeks, review your job log. You might, for example, notice that one of your notations is, "resolved customer complaint." Take a moment to consider what you needed to do or know to resolve that customer's complaint.

Some other examples of the skills involved could include: listening, interviewing, research, paraphrasing, anger management, conflict resolution, or negotiation. By keeping a job log for two weeks, you will have a better and more complete picture of the skills you actually utilize in your work. These can be added to your list of fifty.

It is possible to reach adulthood with your self confidence fairly well intact, but still take yourself for granted. When we are naturally good at something, when it comes easily to us, we may undervalue that skill, talent, quality, or ability. We may even go so far as to minimize our skills because we think they are not valuable or not desirable. This can happen, especially in the workplace, if we do the same job for a long period of time. We get used to it. We get skilled at what we do. It gets easier for us to do it. And, along the way, we may begin to believe that it is not important or that it is not valuable.

Taking yourself for granted limits your options. Everyone has talents and skills that are unique and special to her alone. We may assume that because it is easy for us, it must be easy for everyone to do. Women commonly find themselves with this erroneous mind-set.

Easy Does It

High achievers, those "Type A" individuals, will go one step further, believing that whatever is easy is not worth doing or has no value. They choose to do those things that are difficult for them as a matter of course. When asked what they did well in high school, they may reply, "Oh, I got As in math." But when you look at their college transcript, there are no math classes to be seen. When asked why, they reply, "Well, it was too easy."

In our society, it seems that we have to try harder, faster, and better to feel worthwhile. We value "working hard," "pulling yourself up by your own bootstraps," "overcoming the odds," and "having a strong work ethic." Our attention seems to be drawn to the difficult occupations rather than looking for work that is fun, enjoyable, and easy. It was a major revelation to one high achiever when she, "suddenly realized [that] I don't have to do the hardest thing."

Work is very important to Americans. One of our friends has a sweatshirt that says "I'm Retired. Having a Good Time IS My Job." While that thought brings a smile, it is sad to think that we have to wait until we leave work before we can have a good time. The point of learning more about yourself and developing an accurate picture of your skills, talents, qualities, and abilities is to make the time you spend at work each day as enjoyable and pleasant as it can be. The point is to bring the kid in you to the office, so that you can have fun now and not just when you retire.

A Success Story

Many career counselors and career resource books suggest that you write a detailed story of a success that has happened to you as an adult. We are going to ask you to do this, too.

Pick an event that you are particularly proud of, or that made you feel like you had accomplished something particularly meaningful or worthwhile. Think carefully about everything that went into making this event or activity happen and what your part in its success was. Use the space on the next pages to tell your story. Be specific and describe the entire scenario carefully.

When you have completed writing this story, ask a friend to listen as you share what you accomplished. Ask your friend to add to your list of fifty skills, talents, qualities, and abilities they hear as you share your success story.

My Success Story

What have you learned about yourself in this chapter that will help you develop a more accurate picture of your adult self and the unique aspects you bring to the workplace?

_____

_____

_____

_____

_____

_____

_____

_____

_____

However, despite your new insights, there is still more information you will need to know to create greater career satisfaction. In the next chapter we'll help you identify what is most important to you.

CHAPTER 7

Down to the Core:
Exploring
Your Values

Having our needs met makes us feel comfortable. Having our wants met makes us feel happy. Having our values met makes us feel like our lives have purpose and meaning.

Most of us have principles—a set of "ground rules"—by which we live. They form our philosophy and help us structure both the information we receive from the world around us and our response to that information. These are our personal values and they represent the things, actions, or concepts that are most central to our lives.

Values seem to come to people almost as a "given," as though they were essential truths. Clues about important values can be found in those areas of life where we may feel a sense of obligation, a sense of mission, or perhaps a sense of guilt. You may have read about people who do things that seem remarkable. For example, in the political arena, Eleanor Roosevelt, Indira Ghandi, and Shirley Chisholm all had a sense of obligation about the things they did. It is almost as if they couldn't *not* do what they did because they felt compelled to take action.

That kind of intense feeling comes from your values, and these are important in your consideration of a career. When people sense purpose-lessness or emptiness in their careers, it is an indication that the values they hold deepest are either not being honored on the job, are being violated by the kind of work they do, or are not supported by the culture or philosophy of their workplace environment.

Here are some questions to answer as you begin to examine your values.

Is there something that you feel strongly you have to do during your life? Is there something about which you have a sense of "mission?"

_____

_____

_____

_____

What kinds of things give your life meaning?

_____

_____

_____

_____

Your Core Values

There are values that seem to be essential to our view of the world. These values, sometimes called "core" values, are those that we cannot bend or stretch or violate. They are so important to us that we would never consider compromising them.

Core values might include religious or spiritual beliefs, a concern for the protection of the environment, or a sense of responsibility as a member of the human race. They include the ideas we think of as representing truth, honesty, ethics, or morals. As you consider your values in this chapter, identify those with which you do not want to be in conflict. These are important clues for your career satisfaction.

Write down your answers to the following questions:

How do you think the world should work? What things need to change to fit your image of the perfect world?

_____

_____

_____

_____

_____

What important values of yours are represented by your answer?

_____

_____

_____

_____

Compromise

The values that you hold fall somewhere on a continuum between those that you would never violate and those that can be compromised. In our daily lives, all of us have values that we are more flexible about than others. With these values, it is important to know to what extent they can be compromised. What would you be willing to do? Where would you draw the line?

Having an idea of what is important to you, and to what extent it is important, is an essential part of your career choice and work situation decisions. To insure your satisfaction, you need to have a clear idea of what your limits are within your value system. You will need to consider each one of your career options and potential working environments against your values list.

How do you see the values you have now identified being integrated into your career?

_____

_____

_____

_____

If you didn't "have" to work, how would you spend your time? Be specific. Describe a typical day. You wake up and then what? And after you have finished that task or event, what do you do next?

_____

_____

_____

_____

Working for a company that supports your values can be energizing, fulfilling, and rewarding. Every day can feel like a reaffirmation of what you hold to be right and true about the world. On the other hand, working in an environment where your values are not supported often leads to feelings of frustration, anger, and guilt. Every day in this environment becomes an emotional trial. For example, someone deeply concerned about the effects of pollution on the environment might find it extremely stressful to work for a chemical processing plant. The situation would not support their values.

Expressing Your Values

Values are a part of our whole existence. Women have many options for expressing their values without relying solely on work for their fulfillment. An important consideration then, as you create a list of your values, is to determine what sources you have for fulfilling your values. With this information, you can decide where best to express them.

One area in which to look for clues about your values, especially those related to work, is in the exercise you completed in Chapter Three on your work heritage. Our families are often the main arena where our values are formed and shaped, considered, and reinforced. Look especially at how you answered the statements, "To be a good person..." Here you will find clues about the things that were important in your family. You will find information about what you sensed was expected of you in the world, or at least in your family.

Other clues about your values can often be found in what you enjoy doing—your hobbies, organizational affiliations, the issues you like to discuss with friends, and leisure time pursuits. Consider also the types of books or periodicals you enjoy reading; how you would spend a free afternoon, and other activities that you like to do.

Some people express their values through their families; others through work with volunteer projects or belonging to and supporting organizations they believe important. Ask yourself how you can best express your values. Choose one of the following exercises to complete:

Make a list of the organizations you belong to, the hobbies you have, what you enjoy doing in your spare time, and what you like to read or

watch on television. Then do some brainstorming about what values
these interests express.

Activity   Values Expressed

_____   _____

_____   _____

_____   _____

_____   _____

If you met someone engaged in the same activities as you are involved
in, what clues would this give you about what is important to them?

_____

_____

Defining Success

In the exercise in Chapter Three, members of your family spoke to you
about success. As you look at their answers, what patterns do you see
that have influenced how you define success for yourself?

_____

_____

Write a definition of success for yourself in the space below. Consider
what you would want or need in your life to feel like you are successful.

_____

_____

_____

Clarifying Your Values

Use the space below to respond to these questions: What values do you have? Which of them need to be expressed through work? Which can be expressed through some other activity? (Other activities might include: family, relationships, clubs or organizations, religious affiliations, hobbies, and so forth.)

Values	Expressed Through:	
	Work	Other Activity
_____	_____	_____
_____	_____	_____
_____	_____	_____
_____	_____	_____
_____	_____	_____
_____	_____	_____

Here is an optional activity. List your top five work values below and then answer the question—"How will this value be expressed through my work?" A suggestion for answering the last question might be to consider how your boss might treat you, what kind of product or service you offer, what your coworkers are like, what the mission of the organization is, and so forth.

Value Number One_____

How Is It Expressed At Work? _____

_____

_____

_____

Value Number Two _____

How Is It Expressed At Work? _____

_____

_____

_____

Value Number Three _____

How Is It Expressed At Work? _____

_____

_____

_____

Value Number Four _____

How Is It Expressed At Work? _____

_____

_____

_____

Value Number Five _____

How Is It Expressed At Work? _____

_____

_____

_____

Having your values met can bring renewed purpose and meaning to what you do in the workplace. Remember, however, that values are dynamic and change over time. As we find ourselves in different situations throughout our lives, we notice that what is important to us shifts. Your responses to the questions in this chapter today may vary from those you give in a year, or in five years, from now. Being aware of what your values are and honoring them is vitally important for increasing your career satisfaction.

CHAPTER 8

Beyond the Bare Necessities: Defining Your Needs

As winter's dark days lengthen into spring, many of us start to browse in the yard and garden section of our favorite store, or haunt the displays at our local nursery. While some of us possess a natural talent for growing things, there are those of us who want to grow things, but just can't seem to make it happen. With the best of intentions, we, too, plant our seeds. But somewhere along the line, our efforts break down. Our plants may grow, but they are stunted from the lack of water, sun, or nutrients we have subjected them to. Our gardens are not the lush pastoral scene we see in our neighbor's backyard.

Like seeds and plants, we have needs, too. And to reach our optimum performance and greatest potential for success, our needs must be met.

Unmet Needs = Burnout

Feeling "burned-out" is a sure sign that you have unmet needs. And because you are reading this book, you probably have at least an idea that some of your needs are not being met.

All of us are like seeds when we enter the workplace. We are looking for a place to fit in, to grow, to become all that we can. We take a job that looks pretty good, but we often don't know ourselves well enough to make a good job choice. Or, we fail to honor who we are and rationalize our needs away for a good salary, or because we are flattered to be offered a job, or because we are afraid that there will be no other opportunity.

For awhile, it isn't so bad. But over time, we begin to feel like the seed that is not getting its needs met. Because the job we have does not represent a good "fit" for us, we may actually be doing less than good work. At the very least, we are not doing the best we are capable of. At the worst, we are procrastinating and trying to avoid the work. Our hearts simply are not there.

Clues to Our Unmet Needs

There are all kinds of clues that we have unmet needs. We may feel like something is wrong with us, like we are not being our true, authentic selves. We may find ourselves being more cranky or short-tempered than usual, or find ourselves thinking of ways to "escape." Perhaps we feel depressed and want to be left alone. We may even begin to procrastinate, to use sick leave to avoid going to work, to question our own self worth and our ability to do our job (or any job). Occasionally, we have physical symptoms, like headaches, anxiety attacks, or sore necks. One client developed abdominal pain. She said that she kept hoping that it was appendicitis so that she would not have to go to work for six weeks.

At some point, we start acting out our anger at work. Clues in our external environment then tell us things are not going right. We may be labeled as a "problem employee" and we begin to get poor performance reviews. We don't get the raise that we expect or the promotion that we thought was ours. We start to receive criticism, or get into trouble on the job. We don't have the same level of success that we enjoyed in the past. If we are lucky, we will get fired—if we don't bring ourselves to quit first.

Darlene's experience provides an example of another situation that can arise. In her case, she was not yet receiving external clues or feedback that she was having a problem on the job. But internally, she felt that she could no longer cope with her job as an accountant. She became more and more fearful that she would "lose it" and make a serious mistake on one of her client's tax statements.

She felt like she was struggling to maintain her competent, happy facade at work. She felt like she was being someone else. And she was under a great deal of stress from trying to maintain her "charade." Because no one seemed to catch on to Darlene's turmoil, there was no one to support her and she felt isolated. She actually felt like she no longer fit in with her peers.

Because of her own isolation and lack of support, Darlene began to feel paranoid and to think that people were talking about her at work. At that point, she decided that she needed to explore her career options and search for a new job.

Environmental Impact

Another situation occurs when we accept a job that fits our skills and talents, but is in an environment incongruent with our needs. For example, our supervisor doesn't provide the guidance and leadership with which we work best; there are rules or policies in this particular organization that we find impossible to cope with; our coworkers are not interested in tackling projects as a team and we feel unsupported.

Women often find themselves in this kind of situation: They come into the work force in entry level positions and then are expected to move into jobs where their skills and talents do not match the job's requirements. Frieda's experience shows how this scenario plays out in real life.

Frieda is fifty-five years old and has enjoyed a long, and until recently, successful career in the banking industry. She started as a teller and worked her way up to a supervisory position that she loved in a branch where she felt comfortable. Recently, because of her excellent record in customer service, Frieda was promoted to a new position in the bank.

This new job involves sales, primarily outside of the branch. Suddenly, she is no longer doing what she loves to do—supervising staff in the branch—and she feels uncomfortable in her new job.

Because of this, Frieda finds ways to stay in the branch rather than doing what is expected of her in her new position. Although the expectations of her job have changed, she would rather supervise staff and "run a tight ship" like she did before. She now finds herself getting criticism and poor performance reviews and feels that her self-esteem is at a low point because of the demands of her new job and the criticism she's receiving. Frieda has decided to try career counseling to learn some new tricks to help her cope with her new job so she can survive in the bank. After all, as she says, "I only have ten more years to go." She must re-evaluate her needs and honor them to feel good about herself and her work once again. This may mean that she has to consider leaving this position and exploring other options.

Growing and Changing

We may have a job that fits us well, in an environment that we enjoyed at one point in our life, but find that as we change and grow over time, this work no longer meets our needs. At this point, we can choose to re-evaluate our needs, and our work, to possibly make creative and exciting changes in our career.

Our 20s are usually the age when we are busy exploring our career options. We are testing to find out what we do and do not like in our lives and are more willing to explore career options and to take risks. While salary and benefits are important, they usually take a back seat to other career or life experience-building considerations.

During the decade of our 30s, we want to settle into a career role. We find a company or career that we enjoy, we stick with it, and start to ask ourselves, "Where am I going with this?" Our lives outside of work may also settle into a pattern during our 30s: we may have started a family, be considering the purchase of a home, and have traveled or moved to a new location.

Often the 40s find women asking themselves some hard questions, not only about the meaning of their career but about the meaning of their lives. "Is this all there is?" is a common concern of women in their 40s who realize that they may now want more from their careers and lives than they have in the past. In her career, a woman in her 40s may feel like she has reached a plateau, or she may be unsure of what the next step is for her.

Women in their 50s may start to look toward retirement and think that they cannot or should not make changes in their lives. They may feel that they are too old to be competitive in the workplace. They may rationalize their situation by saying, "Oh well, I only have a few more years until I retire." At this stage of her life, a woman has a great deal invested in her career and family. Considerations about what she wants to do with this investment are important, especially if she is looking toward retirement and contemplating what she wants to do during her mid-life years.

Re-evaluating Our Needs

There are many variations on the above themes and some women face different challenges at different times in their lives. But all of us change as we grow older. Divorce, children leaving the home, moving to another town, family crisis, job (or career) burn-out; any of these events can cause us to re-evaluate our life, our values, or our needs.

For instance, when Marlene graduated from high school, having a career was foremost in her mind and she was not sure whether she would ever marry or have children. When she had completed her Bachelor's degree, she was recruited by a major company and pursued a career path within its ranks. (Along the way she married and had two children.) Now in her forties, Marlene feels that it is "time for me." The children are grown and don't need her as much now. She feels that she has been so focused on the "career executive track" that she has lost sight of herself in the process. Marlene wants to find work that has more meaning for her. She feels that Marlene (the true person deep inside) got lost somewhere in her move up the career ladder.

To get a picture of how to go about fulfilling your own needs, there are three steps you must take: First, identify your needs; then, honor them; and thirdly, negotiate to get them met. We will look at each of these steps more closely.

Identifying Your Needs

Take a few minutes to consider each of the following questions. Then write your answers in the space provided.

What do you need and/or want from a job?

_____

_____

_____

_____

_____

Which of these needs and/or wants are not currently being met by your work?

_____

_____

_____

_____

_____

Some of the typical needs that show up on this list are:

Money   Challenge   Flexibility   Variety

Support   Power   Attention

Respect   Growth   Social interaction   Making a difference

Purpose   Creativity   Independence

Benefits   Room for advancement   Appreciation

Being part of a team   Being influential   Adventure

Similar Values   Someone who listens   Freedom

Visibility   Decision-making   Security   A future

Acceptance   Accomplishment   Helping other people

Diversity   Mentoring

Caution! The needs you listed first are probably the ones that you feel most deprived of in your current job. We sometimes focus our attention on these and let them determine what our next work environment should be like—without considering the other important needs on our list. Focusing on only our *unmet* needs can lead us down the wrong career path and it is important to consider *all* of your needs when contemplating a career change.

For instance, although Dorothy had worked for a major insurance company for a number of years, in a training position that was perfect for her skills and talents, she began to feel unhappy when a new supervisor took over her department. The supervisor was not supportive or responsive to Dorothy's needs and she began to feel incompetent. She knew then that she wanted to get out of the department and find a new position.

When a training position became available in another part of the organization, Dorothy was thrilled because she had worked with the supervisor in that department before and thought the change would be just what she needed. She didn't take time to investigate the requirements of this new position because she knew it was training-related and she liked the supervisor.

Unfortunately, when Dorothy actually started doing the new work, she found it primarily involved registering employees for classes and performing other routine tasks. Dorothy has excellent skills as a training developer and writer, but she did not get to use these skills in her new position and felt frustrated and under-utilized. By focusing on only her need for different supervision, Dorothy ignored other critical aspects of her work—those she needs for complete job satisfaction.

Don't be misguided by your unmet needs into making a reactionary, hasty, "knee-jerk" decision about what you want from your career.

Honoring Your Needs

All of us occasionally would prefer not to go to work. This is natural. But when the feelings of frustration, burnout, anxiety, or just plain not wanting to go to work become chronic, it is time to do an update of your list of needs. This helps you develop a realistic picture of what is wrong. It also helps you decide what specific actions you can take to resolve the situation. When you spend time considering what you really need, and list those needs on paper, they become tangible, not emotional. A specific, logical, and well-defined issue surfaces which you can deal with and work to resolve rather than feeling frustrated or overwhelmed.

Not taking the time to look at your needs, at this point, may leave you feeling vulnerable or emotional about your job situation in the long run. The longer you avoid looking at your own unmet needs, the more you begin to see the whole job as wrong, or you begin to see all of your coworkers and clients as obnoxious, intrusive, stupid, or worse! Your problems at work, and your feelings about them, can escalate—leaving you angry and feeling like you have to quit. However, many times the situation merely involves one or two of your needs which are not being met. In order to remedy the situation, and maintain your sanity and satisfaction, you have to negotiate to get your identified needs met.

Maybe you find yourself saying, "I think that I just expect too much" from a job or career. It is unlikely, however, that you are expecting too much. More likely, your current job is not meeting some of your important needs.

At this point in *Imagine Loving Your Work,* you know which needs are important to you. You don't have to get all of your needs met in the workplace, but your job must meet those which you feel strongly about. You have to acknowledge that you, your needs, and your satisfaction are important enough for you to do something about.

Negotiating to Get Your Needs Met

Bonnie worked in the same unit at a finance company for a number of years. Then, over a period of eleven months, her supervisor and a number of her peers departed and were replaced. Bonnie started to feel that she was burned-out and she no longer wanted to go to work. She decided to take a look at what her needs were at work and when she did, it became clear to her that one of her most important work needs was a quiet environment. She thought about her current situation and realized that the change in staff had drastically altered her work conditions.

Her new peers were gregarious and out-going. They often stood around the office area talking and encouraging Bonnie to join in. Bonnie got more and more angry and upset as she listened to them gossip, discuss movies, or chat about whatever the day's topic was, while she was trying to get her work done.

Armed with this knowledge, Bonnie began to strategize ways to negotiate getting her needs met. When a desk became available in a quieter section of the department Bonnie asked her boss if she could have it. The new location provided her with the privacy and quiet she needed to do her work in the way that was most comfortable for her. Bonnie found that her feelings of frustration and burn-out went away soon after she moved to the new desk!

Sometimes we may think that negotiating for our needs is not something that we can do. When we get to the step where we need to talk to our boss, we start rationalizing by saying things such as "Oh, the company doesn't care how I feel," or, "My boss would never listen to what I need." If we never talk to our bosses, we never give them a chance to help us meet our needs, and we never give them a chance to be different than our vision of them.

It is up to us to get our needs met. It is not your boss's or your company's responsibility to read your mind. Your supervisor is probably worrying about how to approach his/her own boss to get his or her own needs met! When you go to your boss to talk about getting your needs met, take at least three options with you. Pick three specific and realistic ways that your needs could be better met on the job. Present yourself calmly and clearly and be ready to negotiate for what you now know you need from your job. You have to be the one who initiates the conversation. You have to be the one who asks. You have to act to prevent your own burnout.

Doing It Another Way

Practicing clear and direct communication skills enhances your ability to express yourself and achieve the results you desire. But women, historically, have been taught to avoid direct communication, particularly with men.

For example, Marti's mother had an ingenious strategy for keeping the exact nature of her purchases from Marti's father. When Marti and her mother would pull into the driveway after a long, extensive day of shopping, her mother would carefully choose one or two bags to carry into the house herself, through the front door. Then she'd load Marti's arms with the remaining packages and send her in through the back door. Marti's father would see his wife with a couple of bags and think she had been remarkably judicious in her spending. He didn't see the incredible quantities hustled past him at the back of the house. And Marti's mother never enlightened him.

Vicki's mother would buy a dress or other garment, and then hide it in the back of the closet for a month or two. When she thought enough time had passed, she'd pull it out and wear it. If her husband commented on the outfit, something like "Is that new?," Vicki's mother could honestly say, "This? Why I've had this for months!"

Traditionally, women have found personal power through their relationships with men and have had little power in the workplace. Denied control of money, property, and even our own bodies, women throughout history have parlayed beauty, nurturing, and sexuality into paths of power through husbands, fathers, sons, and lovers. We learned to compliment men, to build up their egos, to give the illusion that they were the head of the household—when Mom really ruled the roost. We judged our marriage prospects on who would be a "good catch," a good provider for ourselves and our children.

As a result, whether our relationship was good or bad, we became trapped. We didn't have the education, training, or opportunity to support ourselves in a culture that limited women to the roles of wives and mothers. We were forced to learn skills in manipulation, lying, and deceit to meet our needs. And although the world is changing, many of us have not re-examined our own communication styles and adapted them to current realities, especially in the workplace.

Our lack of experience with direct power, and our education in traditional roles, often leaves us unwilling, or unable, to grasp the power available to us. We wait for our dreams and desires to be discovered and granted and hope that someone will take care of us. These attitudes aren't necessarily bad, but they are not effective in today's workplace. Our challenge is to know our needs and desires well, and then take the initiative to communicate these needs and act on our desires.

Are there needs that you are now aware of that are unmet in your current work situation?

_____

_____

_____

_____

What can *you* do?

_____

_____

_____

_____

_____

_____

So, what happens if you can't get your needs met in your current job? What happens when you are unsuccessful in negotiating for your needs?

Perhaps you need to consider leaving the job you have and looking for another one. What kind of job will that be? The next chapter will help you develop a picture of what your ideal job looks like.

CHAPTER 9

Putting the
Pieces Together:
Your Ideal
Work Situation

Remember a time when you had to find a "special" dress or outfit for an important occasion? Perhaps you had a picture in your mind of the perfect look you wanted to achieve and the price you were willing to pay. You carried that mental picture with you from shop to shop while rifling through the racks of merchandise, to find that particular outfit.

As the time of the event drew nearer, and you became more desperate to find something to wear, you may have started to make little mental compromises to yourself. "Well, it is a little more than I wanted to spend, but it looks pretty nice." "Oh, it just is not quite the color I had in mind, but the collar is interesting." At this phase, you still have some time before you absolutely have to have that outfit, so you keep looking. You start to get discouraged, though, about ever finding the ideal outfit—the one that will perfectly match the picture you have in your mind.

Finally, it is late in the afternoon the day of your important event. You are in the fifth shop you have visited today. Your feet ache. Your head throbs. You look out over what seem to be endless racks of clothing in the wrong color, or wrong size, or wrong material. You are desperate. Your mental picture of the perfect outfit at the best price flies out of your head and you grab the first hanger your hand reaches.

Blazing a trail to the dressing room, you slip quickly into a cubicle. The garment slides over your head. You have to find something FAST. You turn cautiously toward the mirror. Okay, so it isn't perfect. And it's not the color you had in mind. It has a split skirt rather than a straight skirt. It costs $50 more than what you wanted to spend. And the waist is a little bit tight. But, it really is not so bad. Yes, definitely, it will do.

Four hours later, you are in the middle of your special event. For some reason, you just don't feel right. You feel uncomfortable and out of place. The waistline that felt a little tight this afternoon is now starting to squeeze. You know that this outfit was not worth the money, or this party was not worth the money, or you were not worth the money, or something, because you are just not happy.

What happened? You settled for something less than your ideal. You took something that was less than the picture of perfection you had in your mind. You picked something that did not fit. And you feel miserable. The same thing happens when we settle for a job that is less than our ideal; a career that does not fit. Eventually, we feel miserable.

It is easier, however, to get rid of an outfit that we do not like than a career. You can give an outfit to a friend, or hide it in the back of your closet, or sell it at a consignment shop. With careers, we tend to trap ourselves in a specific job or industry and may not readily see options for making a change.

Theme, Fascination, and Medium

When you stepped through the doors of your first dress shop, you had a clear picture in mind of the perfect outfit to suit both you and the occasion. While time and other pressures caused you to compromise this ideal, the picture was still in your mind. Often, we have the same clarity about the ideal career. And then, because of limits and barriers we erect ourselves or have erected for us, the picture changes. We sacrifice bits and pieces of our dream job to meet needs that seem more immediate or compelling at the time.

One way to help ourselves remain committed to our goals is to bring our vision of the ideal career into sharp focus. Think of watching a movie. How long will you remain interested in a film that is out of focus on the screen? An out of focus picture invites us to turn away—it is hard to follow the story and figure out what is going on. The same is true for your career picture. If you are unfocused and unclear about what you are looking for, your attention is more likely to wander and your commitment to yourself is more likely to falter.

A lack of clarity also makes it difficult for other people to provide you with truly useful help and support. If you are unable to clearly articulate what you want, others have a hard time getting a handle on the best ways to provide feedback, job leads, or words of encouragement. Create a focused picture for them, too. Provide examples and specific explanations of what your ideal looks like. Detail what your ideal job duties and responsibilities would be. Give them ideas of the kinds of positions or companies in which you would like to use your talents.

Clarifying the picture of your ideal career makes it easier for you to identify the right job, in the right field, in the right environment, with the right people when it comes along. It's time to draw a mental picture of your ideal, and then fill in the details.

An important part of Valerie's ideal picture was imagining the environment in which she would work. After considering what she really wanted to be doing, and with whom she would like to work, she thought long and hard about what her "fantasy" new office would look like. She described it's location in the building, the kind of desk she would sit behind, where her files would be kept, and so forth. She even went so far as to visualize the ginger jar lamp that would sit on a side table near the door of her office. One day, she went to an interview for a job with a company that she thought she would really like to work for. At the end of the interview, she asked to tour the office. Imagine her surprise when she was shown the office that would be hers if she was given the job, and it matched her mental picture. Even her ginger jar lamp was sitting in the exact location she had pictured in her mind.

While not everyone has such a vivid experience in seeing their visualizations come to life, it is certain that you don't know if you've found your ideal if you don't have a clear, specific, and detailed picture of where you are going. Creating a map for your journey to your ideal will help you chart your course. Your map starts with the following model.

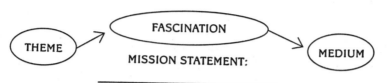

Theme

When you were small, and you were confronted with failure or disappointment, your mother may have provided comfort by reminding you that everyone is good at something, and that you have your special talents, too. These talents, these "gifts" that you have, make you unique and special in the world. They are your essence, and you are better at doing it, or them, than anyone around you. This is your theme.

The word that describes your theme may be one that you have heard teachers, friends, supervisors, colleagues, loved ones, or others use to describe you when they are talking about what is best about you. It is the common denominator of your life. In other words, no matter what you are doing specifically, you observe a pattern of yourself using your theme over and over again. Your theme can be expressed as one word, and it is a word that ends in "er" or "or." (For example: creator, facilitator, sculptor, promoter, adventurer, fixer, planner, communicator, thinker, and so forth.)

People speak of their theme in many ways, but often they say things like, "If I couldn't be _____ , I'd wither up and die," or, "Even if I wasn't getting paid, I'd still have to be a _____ ."

Some people find that they can identify their theme if they are asked to choose one word which describes them to grace their tombstone, one word that would express their essence to those who pass their grave in years to come. When you think of your theme, what word(s) come to mind?

_____

_____

_____

Hint: Ask friends, family, colleagues, peers, and others to help you with words for your list. If you have more than one word, you will usually notice that the list is connected by a common denominator, or relationship. Consider your list carefully to distill the one word that you would choose as your life's theme.

Fascination

The topics, concerns, interests, and activities with which you like to spend your time are what we call your fascination. What do you like to learn about? What is your favorite topic of conversation? If you could read a book about anything at all, what topic would you choose? If you were called to give "expert testimony" in court, what would you like to be an expert about?

_____

_____

_____

As you look back over the classes you have chosen to take (the things you pursued just for fun, or as a part of your elective courses), you will find clues about the topics which fascinate you. You can also find hints in what you are naturally curious about. Do you wonder how airplanes fly? Do you like to fix cars? Do you have the largest collection of recipe books in the neighborhood? Do you know every film directed by Cecil B. DeMille? Can you name all the countries of South America, and their form of government? Do you like to do puzzles? Whether a broad area of interest or a specific topic, your fascination(s) may have held your interest consistently over the years of your life.

Some examples of fascinations are: other cultures, fitness, nutrition, travel, careers, psychology, science, spiritual growth, power, literature, sports, children, or music. What others can you think of? How would you describe your fascination?

Medium

As you consider your life's theme and fascination, the last piece of your map is how and where you express them. This is the medium. Your medium is how the world around you sees your fascination expressed through your theme. When you express them outwardly for money, we call it a "job." Considering your medium, along with your theme and fascination, can provide you with countless career options.

Say your theme word is "communicator." Your fascination is "careers." There are many ways to manifest these in the world, and these become examples of your medium. You could work one-on-one with individuals to provide career guidance. You could lead seminars. You could write career books or create audio tapes. You could create films or television shows about career topics. Perhaps you could work in an employment agency, or work in a personnel office at a major corporation.

As you consider your theme, fascination, and medium, you begin to see that they create an abundance of career ideas. From this information you will also be able to create a mission statement for your career, and your life. Amanda described her theme as being an "activator." She's interested in making things happen, and moving things forward. Her fascination is with other cultures. When she considered her medium, she came up with three options that she liked best: leading groups, coordinating events, and traveling.

Combining these, Amanda decided she'd like to work for a non-profit organization which sponsors international exchange visits. Or, she would like to start her own non-profit corporation leading tours to countries she finds interesting. What are your possible mediums?

_____

_____

_____

Mission Statement

Your mission statement provides a clear definition of what it is you want to be doing in your ideal job. Your mission sums up the relationship between your theme, fascination, and medium, and helps you create a tangible picture of what your ideal looks like. Your mission statement provides a standard against which you can measure and evaluate potential work situations or job opportunities.

Amanda's mission statement, created from the information she had unearthed about herself, became: To increase understanding and appreciation of the differences and similarities of other cultures by organizing and leading groups, creating cultural awareness events, and sponsoring travel and exchange visits. Use this space to create your own mission statement:

_____

_____

_____

_____

Creating a Picture of Your Ideal

With a clear understanding of where you are headed in your career search, you want to have as much detail as possible about your ideal. Defining your career ideal is a way to firmly establish in your mind the picture of what you want and need in your work to both satisfy and make you happy. You have identified your beliefs and values, and noted which ones need to be expressed and realized in your work. You now have information about the skills, talents, qualities, and abilities you bring to the workplace, along with a sense of your mission.

You know which of these you want to use on a regular basis. You now know more about your adult and your natural, child-like self. You know what you need and what is important to you. You are now ready to create a picture of your career ideal, from the data you've compiled so far.

Find a time when you can work totally uninterrupted for a minimum of one hour. You need peace and quiet for this important task. You will want to be able to think about your ideal carefully, considering the information you have compiled and learned about yourself. Make sure that what you write about your ideal is as specific and focused as you can make it.

Close your eyes for a moment and imagine yourself in the "perfect" job. Daydream awhile about this ideal work situation. Spend enough time in this mental picture so that you have a clear idea of what you see for yourself. When the picture is clear to you, open your eyes and write your responses to the following phrases.

Describe what you are doing in your ideal job or career.

Activity	Percentage of Time
_____	_____
_____	_____
_____	_____
_____	_____
_____	_____
_____	_____

Hint: What do you do on a "typical" day? How does the day start? What do you do to fill your time? What equipment or tools do you use? How much time do you spend sitting? Standing? Doing other activities? What are your hours? Which of your skills, talents, abilities, and/or qualities do you use the most?

Refer back to your list of fifty skills, talents, qualities, and abilities generated in Chapter 6. Use this list to determine which skills you would like to use on the job. For each of these, determine what percentage of time you would like to be using or implementing this skill or attribute. For example: "I want to use my skills in public speaking about 20% of the time." You can also find information to help in your Kid Connections from Chapter 5. What does your kid want to do at work? In Chapter 7, you answered questions about how you would like to spend your time. Consider those responses in relation to your ideal.

Describe the environment in your ideal job or career.

_____

_____

_____

_____

_____

Hint: What does your workplace look like? Indoors or outdoors? With lots of other people or just a few? What kind of equipment or tools are around you? Are you in a large city or small town? In a high rise office, shopping mall, warehouse, or other location? Do you drive to work, or take public transportation? Do you travel on the job, or not? Which of your values are supported by your working environment?

Consider both your physical environment and the corporate culture. For example, in your physical environment, you might want to have your own office, or lots of green plants. You may prefer that the corporate culture include a unionized work force, certain communication or supervision styles, a socially responsible attitude, or strong support for the needs of working parents.

Describe your peers in your ideal job or career.

_____

_____

_____

_____

_____

Hint: Do you socialize with your coworkers, or not? What kinds of education and/or training do they have? What is important to you, and your peers? How do you solve problems or conflicts on the job? Do you supervise others? Do you work as a team, or individually, on projects?

Think about the kinds of relationships you would like to have with the people you work with. What kinds of values do they have—are they similar to yours or different? What kinds of people are they? What qualities, talents, skills, and abilities do they have? Are they talkative? Intelligent? Socially conscious? Conservative? Creative?

Describe your boss in your ideal job or career.

_____

_____

_____

_____

_____

Hint: First, do you want to have a boss? If yes, what kind of person would you like to work for? Think about the kind of management style that best suits you. What kind of relationship would you like to have with your boss? How often do you talk to your boss? How do the two of you communicate with each other? Does your supervisor review your work closely, or do you work independently?

How does your boss let you know you are doing a good job? When something needs improvement? What kind of recognition does your boss provide (e.g., raises, letters of recommendation, bonuses, pats on the back, etc.) You can find clues for this answer in your needs list (Chapter 8), in the Kid Connections (Chapter 5), and in the values chapter (Chapter 7).

Describe your customers and/or clients in your ideal job/career.

_____

_____

_____

_____

_____

_____

Hint: Think about what percentage of work time you would like to spend interacting with your customers and/or clients. What types of interaction and/or relationships would you like to have with them?

What do they look like (i.e., clothes, grooming, etc.)? What level of education do they have? What kinds of personalities? What kinds of jobs/careers do they have? What kind of help do they want from you? How do you talk to them? How do they talk to you? How do you interact with them (e.g., selling them something, solving a problem for them, explaining a procedure, answering the phone, and so forth)? When do they interact with you?

Describe your product and/or service.

_____

_____

_____

_____

_____

Hint: Consider the mission or purpose of your organization. What is the use or purpose of your product and/or service? What does it look like? Of what quality is it? How much does it cost? How is the product or service marketed or publicized? In other words, how do you "take it to the streets?" What actions do you take with the product, or what is your role in providing the service?

You Can't Get What You Don't Know

Creating a vision of your ideal brings power and vitality to your dreams. As you think about your new career, and see it play out on the stage in your mind, you have a chance to become comfortable with yourself in a new role, a new image, and a new set of behaviors. Visualizing your ideal is like practicing for your next starring role in the play of your life. You see yourself at work, you imagine how you will interact with your peers, and you start building your own internal credibility and commitment for your new role.

As you continue to visualize and become more comfortable with this picture of yourself in a new career, it seems to become more real. Ideally, you start believing that you really can create this vision for yourself, and that dreams really can come true. Your enthusiasm and excitement at being able to see, and realize, your dreams sparks your motivation and resolve to take action and make what you want happen.

Sometimes, even when we know what we want and can see it clearly before us, we do our best to keep from creating it as a reality in our lives. We think of a thousand reasons that it can never be. We deny the truth of our feelings and clarity of our vision. We tell ourselves that we are too old, or it would be too hard, or we would look too stupid if we chased these dreams at this point in our lives. While we may see more and more signs in our lives that things really do need to change, we cling to what exists for us now and resist moving forward.

One of the most powerful tools for motivating ourselves to move beyond this denial is sharing our dream with someone else. It is important to share our ideal (either by writing it down or saying it out loud) with someone we trust and know to be supportive. Trust your dreams to someone who has no need to criticize and/or limit you. Once your dream is out, and acknowledged, it seems more real. It is harder to retreat back into what you know isn't working for you in your career when you've shared with someone what it is that you *really* want.

You may choose to preface your remarks to your confidante by saying "Don't hold me to this," or "I just want to share this with you, but I don't know if I'm ready to do it yet." It's okay to not be sure you can take action on your ideal immediately. But, sharing it with someone is a vital first step to making your dream a reality. The enthusiasm and support your confidante shares with you will help you start to see your options and feel inspired to take further action. They may even have ideas for helping you get started on your first steps!

Putting a Label on It

Careful! One of the first things you may naturally want to do is "name," or label, your career ideal. You may want to look at your list and immediately say, "Wow! That looks like a financial planner!" or whatever specific role or function you see in your ideal career picture.

We tend to feel most comfortable when we can give our career picture a name. We categorize it and make it seem more "real" because it has a label that we, and others, can understand and relate to. Don't do it! Rather, wait for awhile and stay as open and non-limiting as you possibly can as you develop your ideal career picture. By naming and identifying your career ideal too soon you may limit your options. You may decide prematurely that it sounds like a specific career, and then only look for jobs in that specific field; or examine too critically this ideal you have developed and decide that it simply does not exist as a job in the "real" world. And you get frustrated, or discouraged. None of these responses is helpful for finding your unique career niche and creating career satisfaction. Remain open and non-judgmental!

Now, use this time to continue exploring ALL of your options. Write down all of your ideas; don't limit yourself to only those that seem reasonable or safe, or to those jobs/careers that you know you could do. Stay open to whatever jobs and careers come to mind, and write them all down. What additional ideas come to mind for you?

_____

_____

_____

_____

_____

Getting Feedback

After you have completed your "ideal" description, show it to others to get feedback about what the picture looks like, about what kind of career they think you have described. Ask your friends, your family, your neighbors, your classmates, your coworkers, the people in your carpool, and your business associates.

One client planned a special "feedback" party for her friends and acquaintances. She invited them all to her house and pinned a huge poster describing her ideal up on the wall. Guests were asked to put their career ideas or labels on "sticky notes" and paste them on her poster. Not only did she and her friends have a good time, but she got lots of ideas for many kinds of jobs she might consider.

Another method is to make copies of your list and share them with your friends. Ask your friends to consider what you have written about what you would ideally like to do; then, ask them to share their five (or ten, or three) best career ideas based on your list. You might also ask them to suggest other people you could talk to about your career options.

Selecting Who to Ask

During the feedback phase, avoid asking for feedback from two groups of people in particular. First, do not ask people who occupy "hiring authority" positions in companies where you may want to work. Managers, CEOs, Human Resources professionals, and others who do hiring will try to turn your feedback session into a job interview. They will start to critically evaluate your skills against their needs in particular positions.

Your ideal career picture, therefore, is not a way to do networking for a new job. It is a tool for you to use to make some decisions about what kind of job you want to have. At this point, you are looking for feedback and information only. You are not ready for the new career just yet, and it is premature to use this information (especially in this format) to begin your job hunt.

The second group you should not share your ideal career picture with are those who might give you negative feedback. Many people are unhappy with their work, or with themselves. They will have neither the energy nor the enthusiasm needed to provide you with helpful and supportive feedback about your career options. Your dreams about your future are a precious part of yourself. Share them only with those people who are supportive and helpful.

A Trip to Tomorrow

Another way to motivate yourself to action is to look carefully at the career path on which you currently find yourself, and project yourself ahead a few years to see what might happen if you make no changes.

If you stay in the job you have now, what will your life be like in two years? Five years? Fifteen years? Will you be happy? What rewards will you have gained? What price will you have paid? Will you feel like a success? What will you regret? What will you be doing?

If you discover that this exercise leads you to an outcome that you want, or one that you can be pleased about, that's great. Perhaps you do not need to consider major changes in your career at this time. But, if it doesn't provide you with a pleasant picture of the future, it will provide you with some clues about what does need to change, and what's causing you to resist making those changes. Fear, concern over income or financial security, a lack of training or education, and other issues can be identified in this way, along with ideas for addressing these barriers.

Sometimes, the avoidance of pain is more motivating than the anticipation of unclear, or uncertain, rewards and pleasures in the future. You are looking for ways to support and encourage yourself as you seek to create a reality that is right for you as you formulate a career ideal that incorporates and expresses the best of who you are.

Imagine yourself in the future, about ten years from today. Imagine that you are living your ideal career, and that you are doing the things you described in your ideal career picture. After you have a clear picture of this ideal, use the following lines to write the story of how you got there.

What did you do to get to where you see yourself ten years from now? Consider what you have to do to get there. Write about the transitions you will go through and the changes you choose to make. Use the following timeline to map out the process you follow. This may help you visualize your journey.

Now   5 years from now   10 years from now

There's a difference between having a sharp, clear picture of your ideal and the "job title" or label you might choose to put on it. We suggest that you complete your story vividly and in as much detail as you can, while trying to avoid labeling it with a specific job title. Your goal is creating a visual image for yourself of how your time and effort will be used in your career in the future.

Work with your story until it feels right, and it includes all of the elements that make it ideal for you. With your visualization complete, you are ready to develop the positive steps you will take to move toward your goal.

We are ready now to take a look at the barriers that may stand between us and the achievement of our career ideal.

CHAPTER 10

Move It Out
Of the Way:
The Barriers Between
You and Your Goals

Barriers are those things that separate us from our dreams, our goals, and our wants. What gets in the way of getting what you want? What stands between you and your goals? What keeps you from living the life you were meant to live?

External Barriers

Sometimes, barriers are external. You don't qualify for a particular job because the company requires a teaching credential and you do not have one. You don't qualify for an American Express credit card because you fail to meet the minimum income requirements. You need to earn more money and you want to negotiate for a higher salary, but you know your company doesn't have the additional budget. Structural barriers, however, can usually be overcome.

If you want to teach, you can get a teaching credential. It will take time and resources, but you could do it. You could have the income to qualify for a credit card, but it might mean you would have to change jobs. Instead of getting more money, you could negotiate to keep your current salary while decreasing your work hours, or negotiate for other benefits.

Internal Barriers

Other barriers are internal. These are the road blocks that we set up for ourselves because we think we can do nothing about them. For example, we think that we are not creative enough to do the job we would love to do. We are afraid to make a change or take a risk. We lack confidence in ourselves and in our abilities. Internal barriers can be changed, too. That is what this chapter is about—looking at what gets in the way, what trips you up, what keeps you from realizing your ideal.

Women's Work

Often, the source of our barriers stems from a lack of information—we may have become "foreclosed" about certain careers as a child. For example, Mara always played teacher when she was little. She used to line up her brothers and sisters and cousins in chairs in the yard and make them play school. Mara's family can't remember that she ever played any other games.

Consequently, as Mara grew up, everyone assumed that she would, in fact, become a teacher. And Mara explored no other career options. She had no idea what nurses or neurosurgeons did because she was "going to be a teacher." Mara didn't question her career target; she never considered that there might be another alternative for her. When Mara talks about her choice of a career, she notes that "I didn't really feel that I had much choice. I knew I didn't want to be a nurse or secretary. I tried waitressing in college and knew that wasn't for me. Teaching was really the only other option to consider, at the time."

During the years of Mara's childhood, women had few career options. Housewife-mother, waitress, nurse, beautician, teacher, and secretary were the only work roles considered appropriate for "good" girls. While potential career choices for women have expanded greatly in the past twenty years, many women still initially consider traditional career alternatives in their decision-making process. There are still more jobs for women in clerical, teaching, and nursing professions than in other fields. Our ability to think beyond these roles is limited because of a lack of exposure to information about other career options, about women who work in non-traditional jobs, and about how to pursue alternative career paths.

Our limited view of career options is further clouded by the influence of the media. The roles we see for women on television impact our understanding of what is available to us in the world. What we see women doing, and not doing, in sitcoms, documentaries, movies, and other shows frames our view of where women "fit" in the world. Popular song lyrics as well as the books we read offer additional reinforcement. The behaviors and actions ascribed to the heroines of our favorite children's stories subtly inform us of what is demanded of "good girls," and what happens to "bad girls." We're surrounded by a constant barrage of information that tells us, both blatantly and quietly, what is expected of us in our culture.

Choosing career paths from limited options can restrict your ability to succeed, let alone excel, in the workplace. If you select a career that doesn't suit your skills, needs, personality, abilities, interests, and other important aspects, you set yourself up to be frustrated, ineffectual, and under-appreciated. Your greatest chance for success comes in jobs which you are well-suited for.

Children who have a lack of information about careers, and lack information about their own skills, talents, and abilities, can be "foreclosed" into a career choice, just as Mara was. Foreclosed, in the career development sense, means getting locked into a career choice that may not be best suited to the individual. People who foreclose on a career often stay in that line of work for a long time, although they may actually feel that their job never really "fits" them.

How does this happen? Sometimes parents push their children to live out the parent's expectations, rather than encouraging them to fulfill their own unique potential. Did someone in your family urge you to only consider being a doctor, a teacher, or some other specific occupation? Did your high school guidance counselor, or other significant adult, steer you toward or away from a particular career path?

Some parents, advisors, and other significant people in our lives simply do not know enough about all of the world's career options to help children make fulfilling job choices. If no one ever helped the parent to know and explore themselves and the world of work, they will be helpless in guiding their children in a career selection. If those providing career guidance are not comfortable considering options outside of social norms or traditional roles, they are not able to support an interest in alternative work options.

For instance, although Kim's high school test scores were highest in mechanical and mathematical skills, her vocational counselor had no idea of how to advise a young woman with high scores in these areas on selecting a career option. If she had been a young man, he'd have suggested careers in auto mechanics or engineering, but Kim's situation didn't fit with his view of work appropriate for women.

This does not mean that parents are wrong when it comes to helping their children choose a career. Most of us have never been taught how to make career decisions. Nor have we learned that it is an ongoing, lifetime process. Our lack of familiarity with career options is also compounded by the rapid changes occurring in the world around us. Most jobs that will be available in the future do not even exist today. This makes it tough for us to be expert career counselors for ourselves, much less for our children.

Identifying Your Barriers

From all the exercises and writing you have done thus far, you have learned a great deal about yourself and what part you want work to play in your life. You probably have a good idea of what you want from your ideal career (what would really excite and intrigue you) and you have some ideas about how you can reach your goal.

The following exercise is taken from the book *The Lotus and The*

Pool, by Hilda Lee Dail, Ph.D. The process is designed to tap into the knowledge and wisdom of the right part of your brain. That unconscious part of ourselves holds the key(s) to overcoming many of our internal barriers. Take a quiet moment and close your eyes. Relax and allow your mind to focus on each of the following phrases. When you have a picture in mind, open your eyes and draw the symbol or picture you see.

Draw a symbol or picture below in answer to:

What I Am

On the lines below, describe your symbol picture in words:

_____

_____

_____

_____

_____

Now draw a symbol or picture that answers this question:

What I Would Like to Be

On these lines, describe your symbol picture in words:

_____

_____

_____

_____

_____

_____

_____

_____

_____

Draw a symbol or picture that answers:

What Hinders Me

On these lines, describe your symbol picture in words:

_____

_____

_____

_____

_____

_____

_____

_____

_____

Draw a symbol or picture that answers:

> What Will Overcome the Obstacle

On these lines, describe your symbol picture in words:

_____

_____

_____

_____

_____

_____

_____

_____

_____

Now review your response to the statement, "What hinders me?" in the last exercise. Ask yourself this question, "What are the barriers blocking me from my ideal?" (Go back and look at the list of fears you have accumulated at the end of Chapter 3, if you need help.) Use the space below to write whatever comes to mind.

_____

_____

_____

_____

_____

_____

_____

_____

List all of your barriers in writing, whether or not they seem to be rational. Now, you can begin to deal with these real or imagined barriers and resolve them, one at a time. There is a great line in the film, *Thelma and Louise*. One of the characters says, "You get what you settle for." Addressing your barriers will keep you from settling for less than you desire.

Examining Your Barriers

Look carefully at your list of barriers. Your next step is to find where these road blocks came from. Did you build them yourself, or did someone help you? What is the source of your barriers? Compile this information below.

Barrier   Source(s)

_____   _____

_____   _____

_____   _____

_____   _____

_____   _____

_____   _____

_____   _____

_____   _____

Your list may contain some of the following common fears:

➤ I'm afraid to change because I will lose money and have to sacrifice my lifestyle.

➤ I'm afraid because I don't have the skills I need to really make this change.

➤ I'm afraid because people will think that I'm silly or crazy to want to do this or to leave the "good" job I have now.

➤ I'm afraid that what I decide to do will turn out to be wrong.

Acknowledging the Barriers

Acknowledging that we face barriers, whether internal or external, is an important part of the process. Acknowledging that you have barriers allows you to let go of calling yourself "lazy" or "stupid" for not getting on with it. Acknowledging that there are barriers moves you toward formulating a plan for eliminating them rather than remaining stuck.

Here is an example of someone who moved on. Ella is interested in working with childcare providers on a training plan that she has developed. She has been networking with people she knows in the industry, and she has been given the name of the woman who heads the state child-care agency. Ella has had this woman's name for a month but can't make the telephone call, though she has practiced dialing the number at least a thousand times in her mind.

Finally, exasperated with herself, Ella tries asking the following question, "Why haven't I done this?" She is acknowledging that some barrier is getting in her way. And here are the answers that she received: "If I blow it with her, I'll never get another chance. I don't know what I'm talking about. I don't know what I'd say to her." No wonder she hasn't been able to dial the phone. She is terrified!

Now Ella has a framework for solving her problem. She knows what needs to be done so that she can be comfortable making the call. She knows how to prepare. Here is the list of strategies that Ella developed for dealing with her fear: prepare a list of questions to ask when I call; decide what information I need to get from this person; practice what I will say; do more research, and do additional networking to identify other people I can talk to first who are less threatening.

First Steps First

Although you can decide what step(s) to take, it is usually best to take the most comfortable step first. This is the concrete step about which you can say, "I can do that." It is important to approach that first step without judging yourself or giving yourself unreasonable expectations, or ultimatums. If you find yourself saying, "I should do this" or "I must do this," this is not the first step you want to consider.

Now, turn back to the list of barriers you created earlier in this chapter. Pick one that you would like to explore and write it on this line.

_____

What steps will you need to take to resolve this barrier and minimize your fear and/or risks? List them below.

Risks   Steps

_____   _____

_____   _____

_____   _____

_____   _____

_____   _____

Making Choices

Often the first barrier clients express is, "I can't leave my job." Perhaps you feel this way. The reality, however, is that you *could* leave your job. You could choose to resign tomorrow. But it might not be in your best interest to leave that quickly, or to even leave at all. As you evaluate your barriers, fears, and the risks involved, it is important to consider how your decisions and actions can be pro-active and can thus help you take care of yourself, your needs, your career ideals!

Now is the time to get rid of the "I can'ts." "I can'ts" are about being a victim and believing you are powerless to make changes in your life. Review your barriers list for those statements that begin with "I can't." List them here:

_____

_____

_____

_____

_____

One way you can get out of the victim mode and back into a powerful, pro-active mode is to substitute the words, "I don't choose to" or "I could" for "I can't." Instead of saying, "I can't leave my job" the phrase becomes, "I don't choose to leave my job." See what a difference this makes? "I can't make $50,000 a year" becomes, "I could make $50,000 a year." Making a choice puts you back in control. You are in the driver's seat when you choose to take one action over another.

Change the, "I can't..." statements to sentences starting with, "I don't choose to...," or, "I could...," or, "I could learn to..." on the following lines.

_____

_____

_____

_____

_____

Sometimes our fears are about the "unknown." While we do not know what a new job or adventure will bring to our lives, we do know our current day-to-day routine. And while it may not be the most happy or satisfying, it is familiar and, in some ways, comfortable. We tend to feel the known is better than the unknown, just because we know what it involves.

Taking Risks

Closely linked with our fears and those real or imagined barriers is the element of risk. Risk concerns what we think we have to give up in order to get what we want. Risk is about what we think we might lose in the process, like status or money. Perhaps the risk is getting hurt, or losing face and looking foolish. Sometimes there is a risk concerning physical safety and well-being. We could lose comfort, security, or support.

Our willingness to take risks is based on several factors: our personality; the messages (positive and negative) from those around us that we internalized as we were growing up; our experience of how life works; and our perceptions. We all have the same basic needs in life. Abraham Maslow classified these needs into a hierarchy. At the base are the most fundamental, physical needs for survival—food, drink, shelter, warmth. Next comes safety and security needs. The hierarchy continues to the peak with the highest need—self-actualization.

Maslow's Hierarchy of Needs

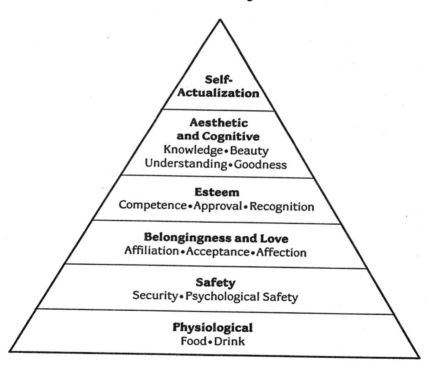

Self-Actualization

Aesthetic and Cognitive
Knowledge • Beauty
Understanding • Goodness

Esteem
Competence • Approval • Recognition

Belongingness and Love
Affiliation • Acceptance • Affection

Safety
Security • Psychological Safety

Physiological
Food • Drink

Because of our varied backgrounds and psychological make-ups, we are willing to risk at different levels. Some folks will risk giving up the approval of others to make a change in their life. Others will not. Some will risk even their physical safety. Think of stunt people, "dare devils," mountain climbers, nuclear plant employees, and others who choose physically dangerous, high-risk occupations.

Only you can evaluate how far down the hierarchy of needs you are willing to risk. Only you can decide what it is worth the risk of jeopardizing, or losing, as a result of the decisions you make. There is no "right" or "wrong" level of risk, there are only individual choices. Being familiar with your level of "risk comfort" is an important part of your career decision-making process.

One technique for imagining the many alternatives involved in a particular risk is to ask the question "What if..." and then visualize all of the ideas that come up in response to that question. You can use this technique to consider how the options could play out, as a way to choose the most effective and comfortable course of action. This technique will help you make a more informed choice of the best alternative(s) available to you. When you have a way to see what may be facing you as you encounter a risk, you have a way to move beyond the fear and take action.

Poised on the Edge

Sometimes, making a decision may seem like standing on the edge of the Grand Canyon. The other side is where you want to be. How do you get there? You could jump off the edge and hope that you reach the other side. Or, you could spend some time considering your options, discovering what alternatives you have, and exploring the resources available to you. The goal is to reach the other side; how you get there is the creative part.

The important point to remember about facing risky situations is that there is always more than one way to reach your goal. Take your time, be creative, brainstorm and list all the possible alternatives. You don't have to take the hardest, scariest step first. Rather take easy, fun, and comfortable steps that you know you can accomplish. With each step, allow yourself a sense of success and achievement as you face your challenges.

Time to Stay or Time to Leave

One of the hardest decisions in career planning is when to leave the job you are in. As you review your barriers, fears, and risks list, you may feel that you are too tired or burned-out to take any steps at all. Perhaps you are concerned that you will leave your current job and move into one that is even more stressful.

You are the only one who can decide when the right time to leave has arrived. You are the one who determines if it is all right to stay in your current job while you are preparing for your next one. You need to identify the degree to which your job is draining your energy or killing your self-esteem. You determine whether or not you will quit immediately or will stick it out awhile longer.

Again, the key is identifying your options. Can you maintain your sanity in your current job? Are there interim positions, perhaps less responsible or stressful, that you could do for awhile? Could you work part-time in your current job or for another company? Do you have the resources to take time out from work? What outside activities could you get involved in to meet some of your needs? Examining thoroughly all your options will help make your transition easier.

Resolving barriers, lessening fears, facing risk, and moving forward all involve making changes in our lives. We start to do things differently than we have done them in the past. In terms of your career, it may mean leaving a company or work team that you have been with for a number of years. It may mean learning new skills.

Let's move on to your plan of action, now that your barriers are out of the way.

CHAPTER 11

Transforming Dreams
Into Realities:
Your Action Plan

Y ou have now invested a great deal of time, energy, and thought in creating a wealth of information about yourself. Some is information that you reclaimed from your childhood; a portion is knowledge about your adult skills and about your talents, likes, and wants. You have developed a sound picture of your ideal work situation, your ideal career.

Formulating a plan of action is the next step in realizing your career goals. To do this, you will determine what steps you need to take, in what order, and by what date. You will set personal goals for accomplishing the steps in your career plan. And, remember the importance of rewarding yourself when you successfully complete each step in your plan! Rewards are an important part of keeping yourself motivated and moving toward your goals.

Patterns and Pieces

As you look back over the exercises you have completed in previous chapters, look at the clues, insights, and important messages your responses provide. What patterns do you see? You began to put the puzzle pieces together in Chapter Nine as you created your ideal work situation. Perhaps you discovered a need to gather more information to focus your career goals. This can become a part of the action plan you develop in this chapter.

The process of breaking your career goal down into manageable steps formulates your Action Plan. For example, perhaps you will need to do more research about the kinds of career options that interest you. Add this to your Action Plan. You will find that doing career research is an important part of your Action Plan. Use your local library. Find information in bookstores. Look at the Dictionary of Occupational Titles which contains over 20,000 job listings. Talk with friends who have jobs that you think you would be interested in. Read biographies about people who have done things you would like to do. Consult the career guidance center at a community college in your area. Visit your local branch of the state employment office. Join professional organizations. Seek out women working in a variety of careers as role models and sources of information on work options.

Perhaps you will need to complete informational interviews with people working in the field of your choice. Maybe you will need to identify companies that hire people with your talents and interests. You may need to restructure your resume to highlight your career-specific skills. Perhaps you will want to read books or attend classes to brush up on your job search techniques. These are all possible steps to include in your Action Plan.

Step by Step

The Action Plan that you develop is a step by step outline of what you will do to move from where you are to where you want to be. It is based on the picture of the ideal that you have developed. The plan also includes the steps you outlined to eliminate the barriers and resolve the fears identified in Chapter 10.

Use the space below to list all of the steps or actions you will take, or the things you will do, to reach your career goal. List your action steps from last to first, so that you are looking at your sequence of events in reverse order.

For example, if you have "career research at the library," "informational interviewing," and "apply for jobs" on your list, you will need to complete the library research before you are ready to talk with professionals in your field of interest. You will need to complete the informational interviews before you are ready to make formal applications. Therefore, "apply for jobs" might be step 8, "informational interviewing" might be step 5, and "research" might be step 3, with other steps interspersed between.

_____

_____

_____

_____

_____

_____

_____

Make Them Manageable

Review your list as you ask yourself this question, "Is this step too big?" You may find that you need to add a few intermediate steps to your list. Is there anything on this list that is too scary? Break these down into steps that feel easier, less fearful, and more manageable. Are there other barriers you have not yet addressed? Make sure to include all of the steps you need to resolve your fears and barriers.

Rewrite your prioritized list below and add a timeline. By what specific date(s) will you complete each step in your Action Plan? They can be small steps, but you need to actively move toward your ideal career goals. You can take as long as you like to complete your Action Plan, but it is vital to begin taking steps immediately.

Action Step	Date of Completion
_____	_____
_____	_____
_____	_____
_____	_____
_____	_____
_____	_____
_____	_____
_____	_____
_____	_____

Was it easy for you to develop your Action Plan steps? Some of the items you list probably will seem easy to accomplish. Others may seem difficult or overwhelming. Perhaps it was difficult to think of the steps you need to take. Some examples of things that could get in the way of creating your plan include: barriers, fears, lack of information, or lack of support.

Gathering Support

As you consider making career changes and proceed through your Action Plan, you will need a process for building a team to support you. Like a sports team that is trying to win the big game, we need to have fans behind us, leading cheers and giving us the encouragement to keep going. It is hard to accomplish goals in life if we have to do it all alone and without moral support. Your search for career answers is no different. It will be easier for you, and more fun, too, if you can share your experience with friends or advisors.

Building a support network to help you through this process might involve finding a mentor or role model in the career area you want to pursue. You will want to build a community around and within yourself that nurtures your dreams and boosts you up when the going gets rough. Remember to be careful with your career dreams. People who are not positive, helpful, and energizing should not be a part of your support team. Sharing your dreams with people who are supportive will help you turn those dreams into reality.

You might want to join, or form, a support group for others in career transition. You can work with a counselor one-on-one, or with a group, by using the exercises in this book as a basis for your self-discovery process.

Starting Your Fan Club

Use the lines below to make a list of the people who care about you and who you can turn to for support. List what you need to get from your support people. Match your needs to the person who would be most helpful to you.

Person   Need

_____   _____

_____   _____

_____   _____

_____   _____

_____   _____

_____   _____

_____   _____

Rewarding Yourself

Make sure that a part of your plan includes honoring your successes along the way. Whether they are small or monumental, it is important to acknowledge and reward yourself for what you have accomplished. Your support team can help you by providing those important "pats on the back" and encouraging words. You can also do some things for yourself.

For instance, celebrate! Have a party for yourself and acknowledge your accomplishments. Every effort is a victory, and it moves you closer toward your goal. It also helps make it easier to take the next step and the next, even the ones that at first seemed too difficult or overwhelming.

When...Then

As the old saying goes, "don't put off until tomorrow what you can do today." Once you have created your plan, take some steps every day (and it is not all right to put off creating an Action Plan as a way to avoid doing something!).

It is not uncommon to hear people postpone some "reward" in their life until they have reached a goal. Have you ever heard a friend say, "Well, I'll buy new lingerie for myself when I lose twenty pounds," or,

"I'll quit this job after I'm vested in the retirement system three years from now."

These are examples of putting off living in the present for some time in the future when things are the way you think they should be. The problem with this philosophy is that our mythic vision of the future often does not materialize. Inertia takes over and we remain the same; we don't take the risk to initiate change. Six months, a year, or five years later, we are left with not only the twenty pounds we had to lose when we made the promise to ourselves to lose it, but the ten more we've gained since.

What kinds of messages do you tell yourself that tend to postpone your happiness or put off living a fulfilling, satisfying life? Do any of your messages fit in these blanks?

"I'll _____ when _____ ."

"I'll _____ after _____ ."

"I'll _____ if only _____ ."

"When _____ happens, I'll be able to _____ ."

Look at your list of postponing messages. What can you do to get on with your life? What steps can you take to embrace happiness and fulfillment now? Make sure these are included in your Action Plan.

_____

_____

_____

_____

_____

_____

_____

_____

_____

_____

Some people are experts at "looking" like they are doing something when, in actuality, they are not being productive. This is a way to hide, put off, or excuse ourselves from reaching our future career ideals. Let go of needing to have everything "perfect" before you can take a step. Let go of non-productive expectations. As the slogan says "Just Do It."

CHAPTER 12

Work Search Skills

T he culmination of your career search journey is being offered the "perfect" job; finding the employer and work environment that best uses your talents, skills, and abilities and that allows you to meet your wants and needs. But how do you make the shift from the picture of the ideal in your mind to a solid offer of a job?

There are thousands of books that describe the skills involved in the perfect job search effort. Many of them are listed in Chapter 15. Rather than offer yet another recitation of the technical skills involved in writing the world's greatest cover letter, we'd like to offer some tips and ideas on what we consider to be the most important aspects of your work search efforts.

Your goal is to present your background, skills, qualifications, and other work-related assets in such a way that you are seen as a qualified, serious candidate for the position you are seeking. Competition for vacancies is often stiff, and your goal is always to be in the group that is left for consideration after the cuts have been made. Every contact with you, whether in person or on paper, should confirm for the employer that you know the industry, know what's involved in the job, and are able to handle what will be expected of you.

For Better or Worse

It seems that the economy is either good or bad, and the state of the economy impacts your ability to find your ideal job. In tough times, the competition is fierce. Employers have more latitude for selecting candidates with an exact fit of skills, experience, education, and work history for their positions. In tough times, your network of professional associates becomes your most important avenue for finding work. Employers advertise less when times are tough, to limit the number of applications they must review. Therefore, who you know can be vital in locating the perfect job.

Remember that only about 20% of the vacancies that really exist within companies are ever advertised to the public, through the newspaper or other channels. This creates a huge "hidden job market," filled with a variety of opportunities you want to have access to. The only way to access these jobs is through networking and personal contact with friends, business associates, professional organizations, and so forth.

In good times, fewer folks are in the job seeking market. Employers become more willing to place advertisements for position vacancies, and to look at people who have transferable skills and abilities. However, your network still remains your best source for information on jobs that are available and for helping you access them.

The Paper Path

Your portfolio is a collection of examples of your work, complimentary things said about you by supervisors or customers, certificates of completed training, or other documents that serve to enhance your resume and other employment materials. Gathering these documents together in one place makes your networking, application, and interviewing process easier.

Portfolio materials can be used to provide graphic illustrations to your verbal explanations of projects, ideas, or innovations you have developed on the job or in other situations. Use your materials to demonstrate the range of activities you have been a part of or abilities you have developed. You can also use items in your portfolio to compliment yourself to potential employers without sounding like you are "bragging." For example, if the position you are seeking requires excellent customer service skills, letters from past clients or customers highlighting your ability to provide quality service can reinforce your skills to potential employers.

Be creative! Think of all of the possible documents or materials you could include in your portfolio. Develop a system for saving copies of the following as a part of your file:

➤ **Updated resume.**

➤ **Commendations, Service Awards, and/or Letters of Recommendation.** Ask customers or coworkers who compliment you if they would mind putting their compliment in writing for you. Include certificates, memos, letters, and other documents that acknowledge your ideas, incentives, safety records, sales, customer service, speed, attendance, and so forth.

➤ **Work samples** of projects, written materials, graphic design, instructional materials, correspondence, or ideas you developed. Include data or reports that illustrate your "track record," i.e., sales volume, number of calls processed, cases closed, and transactions completed.

➤ **Newsletter or newspaper articles** either about work or volunteer accomplishments. Include articles where you're quoted and those about projects on which you worked, even if your name is not specifically mentioned. Keep them current.

➤ **Job and/or position descriptions.** If your job changes, make sure that this document is updated to reflect your additional responsibilities or duties. If you don't have an "official" job description, write one for yourself that reflects your duties and responsibilities.

☞ **Transcripts, certificates of training, and other documents** which indicate you have completed professional development courses, workshops, or seminars. You might also include papers, projects, and other products you developed for your classes.

This list is by no means exhaustive of all the potential documents, samples, and other supportive materials that could be included in your portfolio.

What other ideas do you have for rounding out your portfolio file?

_____

_____

_____

Recommendations

Today's employers receive hundreds, and sometimes thousands, of applications and resumes a year. The cost in staff time to review and evaluate all of these materials is staggering. It can go even higher if employers are checking references or completing background checks. More and more often, employers are asking that you submit current letters of recommendation with your application packet or supplementary materials. Employers use these as a part of their process for determining which applicants will be invited for interviews.

Your coworkers, supervisors, professional associates, and customers or clients are all excellent resources for requesting letters of recommendation. You can ask that they prepare letters for specific position vacancies, as well as asking them to complete a "generic" letter about your outstanding skills and abilities. This will eliminate the need to repeatedly ask them to complete letters, especially if you are applying for numerous positions. When your letter-writing supporters ask about what should be included, either tell them about the specific kinds of positions you are seeking, or about the specific skills and abilities you want to high-light in your job search.

Use a strategic approach. Make a list of the people you will be ask-ing for generic letters. Then, list the skills, abilities, talents, and qualities you possess which you feel are most important in the career or position you are considering. Ask each of your supporters to address different points from your list in their letter, so that you have a collection that reflects a full spectrum of yourself in relation to your ideal.

A Custom Job

For almost any position above entry level, having a resume which out-lines your experience and skills is an important part of the application process. There are many types of formats and approaches for develop-ing your resume, and resources which can help you complete the process are listed in Chapter 15. Here are some points we think are vital to being head and shoulders above your competition.

➤ While it can be time consuming to customize your resume to meet the requirements of the position and company for which you are applying, it is an essential way to present your skills and abilities to employers. After you have worked hard to research the industry, the field, and the employer, it's worth your time to develop letters and resumes which target specific details about the job for which you are applying, or the company in which you would like to work.

➤ If possible, letters should be addressed to a specific staff member and should indicate which position you are interested in, and how you learned about the vacancy—especially if it was through someone within the company or your professional network. (Make sure you include information indicating that you will be following up on your letter to arrange a time to meet.) Use your cover letter as a tool for highlighting the skills, abilities, and qualities you have which would be especially helpful in the position. Your goal is to make the employer's job easy. You want her/him to immediately see from your resume and cover letter that you are worth considering for the vacancy. Paint a picture with your words that will create a clear visual image of you and your abilities in the employer's mind.

☛ Your relevant skills and experience should be easily located and highlighted on your resume. Your descriptions of your previous work should be short and concise, and your resume most often should be two pages or less in length. Use words and phrases that are highly descriptive, specific, and add "zing" to your narrative. Present your work history and level of responsibility honestly. While that means don't exaggerate, it also means don't underestimate and sell yourself short. Your resume is no place for being overly modest; if you supervised 120 staff members or you ran a multimillion dollar program, say so.

☛ While you may choose to have a resume service or other resource person edit and fine-tune it into a final product, we recommend that you develop at least the first draft of your resume on your own. Why? Because writing your own resume helps you get a clear picture of the work you have done and prepares you for the interview process by allowing you to develop ways to present your skills, abilities, and work experience. If you spend lots of money to have someone else develop a resume that you must use to market yourself, you may feel that it doesn't fit you well, or that you are uncomfortable saying in an interview what is listed on your resume. It's okay to get help, especially in the final stages, but your resume should accurately reflect your talents, your work history, and your personality. Ask friends or associates to review your resume and provide you with feedback on it's focus and clarity.

☛ If constantly revising your resume is impossible for you, develop at least three standardized versions that highlight your skills from slightly different angles. This allows you to select your most appropriate resume from the ones you have developed.

Getting to Know You

Although at times we may think of them as a performance, a grilling, or a hurdle that must be overcome, interviews are a *mutual* exchange of information between you and a potential employer. While the company certainly must know information about you to determine whether or not to make a job offer, you must know information about the company to know whether or not to accept that offer.

Ask for the information you need, observe the work environment, ask to meet your potential coworkers, or pursue other issues that are important for you to be comfortable with the company or organization. Sometimes, we get so focused on getting the offer of a job, we lose sight of the day-to-day requirements of the position. Your ego will survive not being offered a particular job, but *you* may not survive getting hired into or stuck in the wrong job, the wrong company, or the wrong work environment.

One of the most important skills you can develop as the interviewee is listening. Listen carefully to the information that is shared with you through the interview. Not only the overt message, but the "question behind the question." Do they repeatedly ask how you deal with stress or conflict? Does this indicate that the position you are considering must confront these issues daily? Do they ask how you feel about certain work requirements? Does this mean these will be conditions for your employment? Observe the work environment, and the relationships between employees. What does this tell you about the company? A wealth of information is available to you throughout the interview process, even while you are sitting in the reception area. Here you will have opportunities to observe how people interact in the company, and gather clues about the mood and environment of the company.

Honesty is the best policy. We've heard this since we were children, and it is especially true in employment situations. Exaggerating our skills on a resume, overselling our abilities in an interview, and fudging on our educational achievements may be tempting, but they can lead to a nightmare. Trying to maintain a lie is too draining to make the initial advantage it provided worth the effort. Get hired for who you are, not some fantasy character you create. It isn't your ideal job if you have to twist yourself out of shape to fit the requirements or to meet the day-to-day challenges of the job.

Meeting Face-to-Face

A recent poll indicates that more people fear public speaking than fear dying—and employment interviewing is public speaking on a much smaller scale. Even the most self-confident and outgoing find themselves getting nervous before interviews. Our hands sweat, our throat gets dry, and the impressive facts of our work history just fly out of our heads. Although we may be skilled and comfortable with our performance on tasks that we do every day, for most of us, employment interviews are an occasional activity and we may be "rusty," and therefore anxious about going through the experience. There's *got* to be a better way!

▶ First, prepare for your interview. On rare occasions, you will be interviewed by a trained staff member, skilled in helping you present your skills and abilities in their finest light. More often, you will be meeting with a supervisor or decision maker who performs interviewing as a part of her/his other duties who may not know the best ways to support you in an interview situation. It becomes your responsibility to make up for the interviewer's deficiencies. If, at the end of the interviewer's questions, there are still points you have not had the opportunity to share, make sure you add this additional information about yourself.

▶ Put yourself in the place of the interviewer. Think about what she or he needs to know about you to make a hiring decision. What's important about your experience? Your skills? Your ability to be a great employee in this job? Write down your answers, and take them along with you to the interview.

▶ That's right—take your notes with you. Many of us have the idea that we must enter the interview room empty-handed, and then speak extemporaneously for the next thirty minutes or an hour. That's not true! Show yourself to be better prepared than your competition by by having notes of the important points you want to emphasize during your interview. Consult your notes, and use the points you have prepared as they are appropriate in response to the questions you are asked.

➤ Keep your explanations and your answers brief and to the point. Often the person who talks most in an interview is least likely to get the job, because the more information you share, the more likely you will trigger one of the interviewer's "red flags." Red flags are those points that will eliminate you from consideration from the position. The challenge for "talkers" is to limit your remarks to what is pertinent and relevant to the question. For those who are not so talkative, the challenge becomes speaking up and including a complete picture of your skills and abilities in response to questions. In both cases, your notes can be invaluable in helping you identify and speak to specific information you wish to share with the interviewer.

One way to organize your thoughts is to use an interview prep sheet which may consist of three parts: Strengths; Questions; and Closing Points. Here is an example:

My Five Strengths for _____(Position).

1. _____

_____

2. _____

_____

3. _____

_____

4. _____

_____

5. _____

_____

Questions to Ask: Reminders:

1. _____   _____

   _____   _____

   _____   _____

2. _____   _____

   _____   _____

   _____   _____

3. _____   _____

   _____   _____

   _____   _____

4. _____   _____

   _____   _____

   _____   _____

5. _____   _____

   _____   _____

   _____   _____

Three Point Close:

1. "When will you have a decision?

   May I call you on _____?"

2. "Thank you for your time, information about the position, etc."

3. "I just want you to know I'm very interested in this job."

Five Strengths

In this section, you will list two personal qualities and three professional skills which are appropriate to the position for which you are interviewing. For each strength, think of at least one specific example of a time you demonstrated this skill or quality. Your examples should be clear and concise and should include information on who was involved, when the event happened, why it occurred, with whom you worked, and the outcome(s) of your actions. Your descriptions of your strengths should highlight your knowledge and understanding of what the position involves on a day-to-day basis. Let your answers reflect your research and networking. Use the terms and jargon of the industry.

Questions to Ask

Bring with you at least five general questions about the company and/or the position that you would like to have answered by the end of the interview. While some information about the position and company will certainly be provided by the interviewer, you must be prepared to ask about important points that are not covered.

Make sure your questions are open-ended, requiring more than a simple "yes" or "no" answer from the interviewer. The company isn't the only party trying to make an important decision as a result of the interview process. You are trying to get important answers, too, about whether this job meets your requirements and preferences. Suggested questions might include: "What are your expectations of someone in this position?" "What would make someone successful in this job?" "Who would I be reporting to in this position?" "What would I be doing on the job during a typical day?" "As my supervisor, how would you describe your managerial style?" "Can you tell me how you see the company growing in the next two years? Five years?" "If I'm working out well in this job, what opportunities would I have for taking on additional responsibilities in this company?" "What is this company most proud of?"

During the interview is NOT the time to ask about salary, benefits, or time off. While you may certainly be curious about these issues, refrain from discussing these issues until a specific job offer has been made. For more information on salary negotiation, see the section later in this chapter (Making a Deal).

Three Point Close

Point One: Waiting for a decision about a job can feel uncertain, as though you are out of control. To help you feel more comfortable with the process, ask when you can expect to have a decision. Ask what the next step in the decision making process will be and if you can call back at a specific time for more information. You can phrase your request as: "I'm in and out a great deal. Is it all right for me to call you back next Friday?" This clarification can be especially important if you are interviewing at more than one company, with the potential of receiving more than one offer of employment.

Point Two: Shake hands and thank the interviewer(s) for their time and consideration, and answers to your questions. Use good eye-contact skills.

Point Three: Leave no doubts about your interest in the job by *saying* you are interested in the job. Don't assume that they know you are interested just because you showed up for the interview. It is at this point that most job seekers fall short in the interview process; they don't ask for the job. If you are not interested in the position at the end of the interview, remember to leave a pleasant impression of yourself with the interviewer. Later, send back a short note indicating that you would like to withdraw yourself from consideration at this time. Your employment path may someday lead you to be in contact with the employer, or this interviewer, again. You want to leave positive and professional memories of your interaction.

The Tough Questions

While every company, and every interviewer, has their favorite questions to ask during the interview process, there are similarities between them all. Here are some examples of tough questions that often are a part of the interview process, and some ideas for developing responses to them for yourself:

"Why should I hire you?" or *"What do you have to offer our company?"* These questions are really asking you to tell the interviewer something about yourself. Consider the five strengths you customized for this position in preparing your interview prep sheet. Make sure you have brought these to the interviewer's attention and provided examples. Formulate your answer around what the interviewer needs to know about your ability to perform the job, and what you want them to know to make a hiring decision. Practice your answers to these questions so that you are comfortable telling about your skills, abilities, qualities, and talents in response to a variety of inquiries.

"Why did you leave your last job?" Some reasons for leaving are easy to share—a promotion, for example. And some—like being fired—are tough to tackle and explain in a short, concise way. Prepare for this question ahead of time by developing a solid, honest response that presents your reasons for leaving in their best light. Be ready to explain the situation, if the interviewer asks for more information. Explain why the event happened, why it won't happen again, and why it won't affect your work on this job. This is not an opportunity to "trash" your former employer. Keep your answer brief and to the point, providing yourself with as much dignity and self-respect as you honestly deserve to maintain in answering what can be a difficult question.

"What is your greatest weakness?" While we are convinced that this is one of the most worthless questions ever developed by interviewers, it is one that is commonly asked. So, prepare yourself. You can choose to

respond with a "fault" that is really a strength. For example, you are interviewing to be a bookkeeper. You might say, "My greatest fault is my incredible attention to detail. I just have to be sure that all of the i's are dotted and the t's crossed in my work." While you have described yourself as faulted, you have focused on a "fault" that is actually highly desirable in a bookkeeper—attention to detail.

Or, you can choose to disclose a fault that would have no bearing on your performance in the job for which you are interviewing. For example, you are being considered for a swimming instructor position. You respond, "Well, my greatest weakness is filing." Here, you've responded to the question, but not raised any of the employer's "red flags" for disqualifying you from the job. Depending on the interviewer, this approach may allow you to lighten up the tone of the interview by injecting some humor into the proceedings. This might ease tension and make your interview experience more pleasant.

Lastly, you can describe something that has been a shortcoming in the past, but which you have overcome. Perhaps you once were terrified of public speaking, but now feel more at ease in front of groups. Sharing information on how you have confronted your problems head-on and taken action to correct them reflects positively on your ability to problem solve on the job.

"What is your salary history?" When you are asked this question directly, either in response to a position announcement or in an interview, it is difficult to avoid a direct answer. If it is asked as part of your response to an advertisement, respond honestly with the information requested. You must know, however, that this uncomfortable question is used to screen applicants. Whether you have earned too much, or too little, in comparison to that offered for the position, you risk being rejected as not having the "correct" answer.

If you are asked to name the salary range you are seeking, any specific dollar amount response puts you in a no win situation: either asking for too much (more than the employer was considering or willing to pay), or for too little (shutting yourself out of earning a higher salary or better benefits). At this point, it is better to turn the question back to the interviewer. Ask, "What do you usually start someone at in this position?" Or, you can say that a specific salary level is not as important to you, at this point, as the complete package being offered. That complete package includes the job itself, the salary, the benefits, your opportunities for personal and professional growth within the company, and your future career goals.

Thank You, Thank You, Thank You

Although Blake had consistently applied for four or five jobs every week, and occasionally was interviewed, she just couldn't seem to land a job offer. When she discussed her dilemma with friends, one asked if she was following up on her applications and interviews to keep employers aware of her interest in the job. The next day, she started making follow-up calls to the employers for whom she was most interested in working and on her third try, she got asked to come in for a second interview. After the interview, she dropped off a thank you note, highlighting her qualifications for the job, to the employer. Two days later she was offered the job and she accepted.

When Blake asked her new employer why the job had been offered to her, she was told that out of fifty applicants for the job, she was the only one who had followed up with a phone call and a note following her interview. He was impressed with her level of enthusiasm and professionalism, and felt these would be a plus in the position for which she was hired.

One of the areas where job seekers consistently fall short is in following up after the interview. Perhaps we think that if the employer wants us, they'll call, and there's nothing we can do until the decision is made. Perhaps we are frightened to call back, in case we didn't get the job. Perhaps we just don't know what to say when we call. Refer to the work search skill books listed in the reference section for hints on preparing effective interview thank-you notes and follow-up documentation.

Here are some additional tips for letting the interviewer know you are interested in the job.

➤ You can use thank-you letters as one of your marketing tools by using them to reiterate or highlight important points you made during your interview. Or, you can use them to make reference to information you forgot or neglected to mention during your face to face meeting. If you want the job, make sure your letter reflects your enthusiasm and interest in the position, and that you ask for the job.

➤ Thank you notes for interviews should be dropped off in person, or faxed, soon after your appointment. Like other business decisions, hiring choices get made quickly, and you want the employer to know of your interest in being offered the job. Use the letter to show your enthusiasm and interest in the position, along with reinforcing your ability to handle the job. Once again, ask for the job. As with cover letters, give the employer information on when you will be following-up with a phone call (as arranged in the three point close). If possible, include reference letters which reinforce your skills and abilities related to the job, or send along a list of three to five professional references the employer can contact.

➤ As a part of your follow-up efforts, letters of recommendation can also be dropped off in person to the employer with a note which reminds them you still exist and are interested in their vacancy. Your note might simply say, "I'm still interested in the _____ position. I thought these might be helpful to you in your decision making process. Thank you." Use your letters creatively to enhance your personal marketing strategy and to say things about yourself or highlight experiences that you might never have the courage to share yourself.

Keeping It All Straight in Your Mind

Maintaining your own records of where you have applied and interviewed, with whom you have spoken, and about what you have completed career research can be a tedious and time consuming task. While you do not need elaborate forms or data systems to track this information, it is important to develop some system for storing and retrieving important names, numbers, and facts when you need them. Nothing is more embarrassing than getting a call for an interview for a company or for positions you can't recall ever hearing of before.

Keep a copy of any applications, letters, support materials, or other documentation you provide an employer. This will be important information to carry with you to your interview appointment. Store it with information you receive about the company, e.g., position descriptions, annual reports, brochures, and so forth.

Making a Deal

Your research and preparation have been completed. You know what you are looking for, you've made it through the daunting process of submitting your resumes or applications, you've talked to employers and presented your skills and abilities carefully at your interview and you hope you will get a call offering you the position.

How do you ask for, and get, the salary you want? As a general rule, it is best to wait to discuss salary and benefit considerations until you have been offered the job by the employer. At this point, they want you and have expressed a definite interest in making you a part of their team. Waiting until you have the offer of a job gives you a position of greater power and assurance for salary negotiation.

Although you should show your excitement and enthusiasm for the position, also understand that just because a position, or salary, has been offered doesn't mean you have to accept it on the spot. Ask for time to think over your decision, to consider the impact of the offer as you make the important decision to negotiate, accept, or reject the job.

Make sure that you and your new employer have come to a mutual understanding of pay increases, benefit considerations, and other perks that are a part of the job offer. It is up to you to make sure that these issues are clearly spelled out and well understood before you begin employment. If you didn't find out all of the important information up front, you have no one to blame but yourself if there are surprises later.

You should also have done an objective evaluation of your financial needs. What level of income do you need to have to support yourself?

Your family? Your other obligations and responsibilities? What kinds of benefits are the most helpful or meaningful to you? By accepting this position, what new expenses will be added to your monthly budget, e.g., dry-cleaning, parking, meals or business entertainment, uniforms, tools, transportation costs, and so forth. No matter how perfect the day-to-day duties of the job may sound, if it doesn't pay the bills, you won't be satisfied, or employed, for long.

Doing salary and benefits research is an important part of preparing for the negotiation process. Use your professional network to get feedback on the "going rate" in the industry for the kind(s) of position you are considering. Get an idea of what a realistic salary offer might look like. Read business journals and other trade publications that provide information on salary levels in your city. Having a firm idea of what is reasonable and customary in your industry helps you know if the offer you have received is consistent with what others are paid, and commensurate with your experience, skills, and needs.

Make sure that what you ask for in terms of salary, benefits, and other perks is what you want, either as a specific amount or an acceptable range. If the employer counter offers with a lower figure than what you have asked, don't say "no" on the spot. Consider your options, consider the whole package, and then determine to return with another offer or decline the position. The worst that can happen is that the employer will say "no," and the best is that you'll get what you ask for!

If your potential employer cannot offer a great deal of flexibility in terms of actual salary dollars, you can ask for other perks and considerations. These might include the option to work at home, flexible or reduced hours, memberships in professional organizations, subscriptions to trade papers or journals, child care, family leave, or educational assistance and training.

Meeting a Particular Need

Your ideal job, the one that takes advantage of what is best about you, may not exist in the companies where you would most like to work. But, your networking and research tell you that these companies need your skills and abilities. It's possible to develop a position proposal to present your ideas and create your ideal job.

The key to successful position proposals is being able to show that you understand completely the goals of the company, and that hiring you would provide that company with a way to meet those goals by eliminating their existing voids. Use the proposal as a way to paint a picture for the employer of what you would do on a day-to-day basis to benefit the company. Show how your presence would enhance the company's operations and solve their problems. Make sure you are on target with your suggestions, and provide an outline of the actions and strategies you would employ in your newly created position.

Include samples of your previous work, examples from your portfolio, or suggested materials you develop to resolve a specific concern or fill a gap. Your goal is to show your knowledge of the specific needs of the company and your ability to "hit the ground running" in your proposed capacity.

Creating your position proposal is a great way to open up new opportunities within companies. Knowing what you want and what you can do, and how this matches the employer's needs, is the key to successfully using this strategy to create your career ideal.

Maureen wanted to break into a company where she knew there were no current vacancies. She had talked with the company president and learned about the products they currently were marketing. She knew the company was interested in developing additional lines of consumer software and she wanted to be a part of their development team. Skilled as a computer software designer, she first conducted research through her network of professional contacts and industry insiders. After she felt she had identified a gap in her potential employer's merchandise line, she decided to try a bold move to demonstrate her skills, and how valuable she could be on the company's payroll.

On her own, Maureen developed a proposal for a software program that would complement, and enhance, the company's current catalog. She created mock-ups of promotional and other support materials to explain her proposed product. She developed sales projections and showed how her product could make money for the company. Then, while the company president was away at a seminar, she made arrangements to have the materials she developed set up in his office. Upon his return, he encountered Maureen's display in his office. He was amazed. He was impressed. And Maureen got offered a job.

Creating a position proposal can be risky. If you develop great ideas and present them to a potential employer, there is no guarantee you will get a job. It takes courage to put yourself on the line like Maureen did. But it can result in fabulous payoffs and opportunities you might never have had if you hadn't taken the chance.

Using these techniques will move you into the career of your dreams, and into a job that will bring you the rewards and satisfaction you deserve.

As you have followed the *Imagine Loving Your Work* process, you have moved step-by-step toward your career ideal. In the next chapter, we'll look at the alternatives that may present themselves as you develop your career action steps: interim employment, education, and going into business for yourself.

CHAPTER 13

Detour Ahead:
Alternative Routes
To Your Career Goal

areers can become self-perpetuating if you aren't careful. When you consider what your work life looks like, it is often something like this: You start work in a particular industry. Your peers and coworkers are in the same industry. Your professional associates, whom you meet in networking or other meetings, are all in the same industry. Because you are bright and conscientious, you do a good job. You get promoted and have more responsibility. You learn more about your industry. You get promoted again.

It doesn't take much of this kind of momentum before you are so thoroughly involved in your industry that it is hard to move into another career. With your years of experience, you develop a solid reputation and an income to match. Your work brings you a high level of credibility in your field. You become an expert at your job. But you aren't happy, and you want and need to make a switch.

It may be time to consider not only a new job, but an entirely new line of work. Perhaps your employment experience hasn't provided you with the opportunities and challenges you had hoped for, and you are now thinking of returning to school to enhance your skills or prepare for another career. As you consider your ideal and research your options for realizing your dreams, it may become apparent that additional training and/or education are really necessary for you to move forward toward your goals. This chapter will give you ideas for exploring your educational options, considering interim employment, and/or starting your own business.

Leaving the Straight and Narrow Path

For many women, finding another employer to work for isn't the best answer to their career questions, finding ways to create and develop self-employment fills the bill. Discovering your skills and abilities, talents and goals, may ready you to take steps to become an independent contractor, franchise or small business owner, or free-lance worker. More and more women are looking at these kinds of options and deciding they meet their career needs.

While the shortest path between "A" and "B" may be the direct one, it isn't always the best. You can bridge the gap from where you are to where you want to be in your career in many, many ways. While no way is inherently better than another (they are simply different paths toward your goal), the focus of your energy must be on considering your alternatives and charting a course that best suits you and your needs. The best career path is the one that honors your wants and needs, optimally supports you, and allows you to move forward comfortably and steadily toward your dream.

The In-Between Job

There are times when considering a career change feels like taking a scary leap off of a giant cliff, usually into a dark abyss of "the unknown." Faced with the fear and trepidation that such a move brings to mind, let alone its impact on the pocketbook, it's no wonder that many people never change jobs voluntarily or move toward what they'd really like to do. In all aspects of your career change, it is important to make your steps easy and manageable. Considering interim employment is one way to ease the transition process and to create a set of stepping stones along your career path.

Interim employment includes any work you do in your progress from where you are now to where you would like to be in your career. It can be full or part time, in or out of your career field, paid or volunteer, short or long term. While you might include interim employment as a part of any career change plan, it is particularly helpful if you are considering a major shift in your employment; i.e., from one field of work to another.

Deciding how to choose interim employment starts with a detailed appraisal of what you know and what you don't know and need to learn to function effectively in your ideal career. When you have a clear picture of what you need to learn, you can start to develop a plan for how to go about developing this knowledge.

One way to begin to move toward your career goal while decreasing your involvement in your current employment, is to reduce your work hours. You want to start doing *less* and *less* of what you do now, and *more* and *more* of your ideal. Negotiate with your employer to work less hours per week, perhaps starting with a reduction of one or two hours and expanding this over a period of months. Use the time you create to find part-time work in your ideal career field, attend classes, volunteer, join professional organizations related to your new goals, start your own business, or attend conferences or other activities related to your ideal. It may be six months, and it may be six years for a major career shift, but making progress toward your ideal is what makes you a success, not the amount of time it takes.

Turning Down the Heat

Another way to use interim employment as a path for changing your career is to continue to use your current skills, but in an environment that you find less demanding. Perhaps your current job is very stressful, or requires hours and hours of overtime. Maybe you feel pressured to compete with others or meet deadlines. Perhaps your job requires you to spend too much time engaged in activities which you don't feel prepared for or you lack interest in.

Interim employment situations can allow you to turn down the intensity level of your career, while leveraging your existing skills to provide you with a certain level of income and security. Staying in your current field, but taking a step down (for example, from supervisor to production worker) or moving to another department (from emergency room clerk to insurance billing clerk) can help you decrease your stress by eliminating some of your responsibility, emotional involvement, and/or time commitment. Job sharing, working part time or for a part of the year, working at home, consulting, taking a leave of absence, accepting temporary or seasonal jobs, or working two jobs are all possible ways to adjust your work to support your career change goals.

Or, you can find employment that is totally unrelated to your current career field. Perhaps your stress level has been so high that you feel the need to take a break. You want or need to be employed, but you desire something that is more pleasant, enjoyable, or fun. This type of interim employment provides you with structure and helps keep you in the world of work—relating to others and reducing isolation. It also can give you time to recover and heal in an environment that is less demanding mentally, emotionally, and professionally.

The "Short Timer's" Attitude

All of us want to be good employees. We want to do our best, and our employers want us to do our best, no matter what we are doing. But sometimes this attitude can get us into trouble, especially in interim employment situations.

While it is important to meet your obligations to your employer, and fulfill your role as a good employee, it is also important to develop an appropriate attitude toward interim situations. These are jobs that you take as a means to an end; to recover your energy and zest for work, to support you while you attend school or start your own business, to allow you to move forward in your career. You can still be a good employee while keeping a realistic perspective on the situation and its role in supporting you to reach your larger goals.

"Short Timers," those who are leaving a job, are known for having a rather non-committed attitude toward the waning days of their employment. They may still perform their duties competently, but they become detached and limit the emotional energy they channel into their job. This is the same approach you might adopt for your interim employment situations if they are not directly related to achieving your career ideal. You are there to do a good job, and will perform to the best of your ability, but it isn't the most important thing in your life.

Entering into an interim employment situation is a part of your larger career goal. It may not even be in a job or area in which you have a strong desire to achieve. Therefore, it is important to keep your sights on your goals, and not be swayed by feedback about your work performance.

As we have mentioned before, most women learn to please others as a part of their lessons about life. We are sensitive to the feedback we receive and adjust our actions to meet the expectations of our boss, peers, and coworkers on the job. In an interim situation, you have accepted a position that probably is not highlighting the best you have to offer, and keeping this in mind when you receive feedback is important.

Why? Because over emphasizing negative feedback can damage your self esteem and lead you to question your competence. Taking critical feedback personally can erode your commitment to your career ideal. You want to continue to move forward toward your ideal, not back. This job is a means to an end, not an end in itself, for you.

Conversely, over-reacting to positive feedback can also lead you astray. Because you desire to do good work, you do a great job and your boss notices. You get compliments. You get a raise. And, at some point you get offered a promotion. Unfortunately, it's not a position even remotely related to your career goal, or to what you know you really want to do.

Darci encountered this situation when she decided to leave her job in insurance and return to school to complete her Master's degree. She accepted an interim job in a women's clothing store to support herself while she attended classes. Darci knew she had no desire to make this her lifelong career, but she also knew that it was an environment she enjoyed and that her hours would be flexible to accommodate her school schedule. Darci's supervisor soon recognized her as an excellent employee, and started asking her if she would consider a promotion to a position in store management. While Darci was flattered by her boss's support, she knew it was not an offer she cared to accept.

Whether the feedback is positive or negative, you are vulnerable. Keeping your career goals clearly in front of you, and considering the feedback you receive about your interim employment in light of your goals, should help you maintain a realistic perspective. Keep your focus on what you are creating for yourself, and on the supporting role this job plays in seeing that dream shape itself into reality.

Hitting the Books

As the world around us becomes more complex and technologically advanced, education and skills training becomes increasingly important for career advancement. As you read job announcements and position descriptions, you will see that many positions require college degrees and/or specialized skills training to meet the minimum qualifications for the job.

Perhaps realizing your career ideal will require additional course work or completing a college degree. Your first step should be determining if this is actually true, and if so, exactly what courses, programs, schools, or classes you should consider.

Your best source of information on what is really needed in the workplace are professionals who are already employed in the kinds of jobs you would like to do. Talk with academic and admissions counselors at community or junior colleges, universities, or vocational schools. Speak with people doing the kind of work you want, asking them about their own educational preparation for their career and about alternatives for reaching your goals. Use the opportunities presented by networking in professional organizations to find out about the kinds of requirements you face in seeking employment and being competitive in your chosen field.

A note of caution about the information you receive: It is human nature for us to believe that the way we prepared for our job is the "right" way. Try and talk with people who prepared for their employment through formal education and/or training as well as those who "came up through the ranks." You may hear very different information on how to prepare for the career of your dreams. But, both groups can give you valuable insight into what it actually takes to prepare yourself to handle the day-to-day responsibilities of the job.

Feedback from the sources above will help you outline an educational plan. You may discover that you can select specific courses from a variety of sources to supplement your experience, rather than entering a standardized course of study at a college or university. Or you might discover that you need extensive education to qualify for certification or licensing required in your new field.

If additional course work appears to be in your future, make absolutely sure you know what you want and are prepared to go after it. Attempting school after being away from classes for a period of time, while trying to juggle your personal, family, and work needs, can be tedious, expensive, exhausting, and overwhelming. One of the best moves you can make for your career can come to be a hated and despised part of your life, at least for the time that it takes you to complete your course of study. Of themselves, these are not reason enough to avoid classes if you want or need them to meet your career goals. They are merely reasons to make sure you really want it before you start.

Choosing an Educational Institution

Although there are many alternatives for enhancing, building, or completing your education (private colleges and state-funded universities;

private vocational schools; junior or community colleges; company-sponsored classes or workshops; seminars and lectures; self-study courses), as you research the educational requirements for your career ideal, you may find that there are really only one or two options that will provide you with the experience you need. Or you may discover that there are more options than you ever realized. Much depends on the resources available in your immediate vicinity, or your ability to be mobile to take advantage of opportunities in other areas.

Your goal is to choose an environment that supports you to be successful as a student, and helps you move forward toward realizing your dreams. As you consider your educational plans, and try to find the program or classes that will best fit your needs, we suggest that you consider the following questions or issues. When you have an idea of the best learning environment for you, your answers to these questions will make your decision about choosing an educational program easier.

Is the program targeted toward older or younger students?

If you are considering a mid-career change, you have different learning needs and educational goals than "traditional" college students (young people in their early 20s). You need to consider finding a program that supports non-traditional students; one that has more flexible class times that are employment compatible, streamlined registration procedures, time payment plans, and other options.

Can you qualify to receive credit for your work and life experiences?

Many institutions allow students to apply for course credits based on significant work and/or life experiences. Working with an advisor, you may earn credits by completing projects or papers which outline your experience(s) and your learning.

What are the faculty members' qualifications?

If you want a program that is focused toward practical, every-day business applications, you need to select a program whose faculty works with and understands business, whatever your field of interest. (Some colleges and universities maintain a more academic focus for their instruction.) To determine the qualifications of faculty in programs you are considering, consult the course catalog or talk to the institution's staff. You'll find that there are numerous ways for faculty members to keep abreast of what's happening in the field. Perhaps they do consulting with employers in your area, or they teach evening classes while being employed in professional positions in their field of expertise. Are they seen as leaders in the field? Have they published articles or books? Are they completing research?

How will your learning be measured?

Most of us are familiar with memorizing facts and details in order to perform on a test. But, as we mature in our careers, mere memorization becomes less important to us than learning through experience. Does the program you are considering support experiential learning through research, internships, work experience, or writing papers? How will your progress in the course be measured? How will you receive feedback about the areas where you excel and the areas where you still need to do more study?

Does the course of study, and the expense, fit with your plans?

Because of family obligations, or work responsibilities, or any of thousands of other factors, many of us do not have the desire or the financial resources to devote our efforts full-time to completing our education. Your goal in researching your educational options is finding the program that offers you the best education for your time and money. This may not be a "traditional" four year degree.

Some colleges now offer "degree completion" programs. These help people, who have earned some college credits, complete their undergraduate degrees at an accelerated pace, often at off-campus locations. Perhaps you can get the classes you need through your local community or junior college more quickly, and at less expense. Private vocational schools or colleges may offer skill-specific programs that meet your career needs.

Are you ready to tackle going back to school?

Re-entering school can be daunting if it has been a few years since you were a student. Re-learning study skills, how to take notes, remembering strategies for preparing for tests or completing research papers, and incorporating classes into your daily schedule can be difficult if you haven't done it in awhile.

Consider starting small, and adding more and/or more difficult classes as you once again become accustomed to being a student. Start with a single class at the community or junior college level. Choose something that seems fun and interesting, but will also provide you with a challenge. Test your wings here as a way to relearn how to be a student, then build on your success by transferring to a college or university to complete your course work.

It's Not Just the Classes

Learning for the joy of learning is a wonderful experience. It can be exciting to meet your fellow students, to experience new ideas and viewpoints, to expand your knowledge, and add skills to your repertoire. But you can enrich your learning experience and make it more meaningful by linking it tightly to your career interests and keeping a focused perspective.

As you clarify your goals, and pursue educational opportunities to make them a reality, incorporate your career ideas into your papers, research projects, internships, and other assignments. This helps you create materials that can become a part of your professional portfolio and will be valuable as you contact employers and seek employment. It also helps you become even more knowledgeable about your field of interest. The more you learn, the more valuable you will be in your new career.

Hopefully, an important part of your educational experience will be the new contacts you make with instructors, classmates, and others interested in your field. You will have many opportunities to meet and develop positive and supportive relationships with others who share your interests, and who can be helpful in attaining your career goals. Use your academic career to build professional relationships, and don't forget to ask your instructors for letters of recommendation.

It's important to keep your focus on what you know is right for you, and to consider all feedback in light of how it is offered. Just because someone shares your interests doesn't mean they are in the "right" job for them! Appraise your experiences, and other's feedback, realistically. Keep your perspective and your energy focused on creating the work you desire.

It's All Yours: Starting Your Own Business

Striking out on your own to create your own business can be exhilarating, terrifying, gratifying, exhausting, and overwhelming. But Americans thrive on the entrepreneurial spirit. According to the Small Business Administration, women will own 40% of small businesses by the year 2000.

Many of us dream of finding just the right product or service to help us achieve fame and fortune or just become our own boss. If starting your own business is a part of your career ideal, it is important that you choose your business venture carefully, and that you have done your research so you know what you are going to face. There are important jobs to be done in all aspects of society, and you will find your greatest satisfaction not in molding yourself to the needs of a so called, "hot" job, but in molding a job in an industry that suits you. Hot jobs are only hot for those people suited to them.

Patricia Aburdene and John Naisbitt, in *Megatrends for Women* (Villard Books, 1992), say the following about hot jobs:

What are your needs, talents and desires for creative self-expression? In the practical matter of choosing one's work, we believe the best advice is to follow your heart and be "impractical." People who love their work have a better chance at success. And if the projections of economists (or trend forecasters) are wrong, you have not wasted time on a job that is boring as hell. (p. 64)

Our fantasies about starting our own business often focus on the more exciting and glamorous aspects of the process—making a big sale, traveling to exotic places to meet important clients, being named "Business Owner of the Year" by the Chamber of Commerce. But because of the time, energy, and financial resources that starting your own business requires, it is absolutely vital that you choose a business that fascinates you and is suited to you. You'll be spending a great deal of your time with your business. What will it be like? Ask yourself, "Why do I want to do this?" (An answer that indicates a desire for short-term gain, particularly financial, is a clear sign that you are not ready to start and maintain a small business.)

Instead of taking a long-term view, many budding entrepreneurs think in terms of "Where can I make a fast buck NOW?" The result of this attitude is a multitude of small businesses opening and closing in rapid succession in store fronts throughout our communities. Frozen yogurt shops, mail centers, flavored popcorn shops, work-out gyms, and other "trend" shops have followed this pattern.

For instance, when Margeaux began investigating small business opportunities, instead of examining what she really liked and didn't like to do, she looked at hot trends. And what she kept hearing about were video rental stores.

While she wasn't wild about movies, she thought she was on the right track because she really enjoyed the process of getting her business set up and ready to open its doors. What Margeaux didn't figure on was hating the day-to-day work in her video store. She quickly came to loathe getting movies off the shelves, restocking the store, and interacting with people all day long. She didn't like movies nearly as much as many of her customers, who wanted to chat about old movie trivia on their visits. While she had enjoyed the up front process of opening her business, she hadn't given enough thought to what she would actually be doing on a daily basis and whether this would fit with her personality, her skills, and her needs and wants. Finally, it just became too much. With business falling off and her resources depleted, Margeaux was forced to close the store within one year of her "grand opening."

Some small shops make it—the shops which are opened and nurtured by people who truly love their business, and who have found a niche for meeting their career and personal goals. As you begin to put together your strategy for developing a business, make an honest and realistic appraisal of yourself. What are you good at? What strengths do you bring to your business venture? What will you enjoy doing? What will you find tedious? What do you know how to do? What will you need, or want, to hire someone else to do for you?

While all of us have talents, most of us are not able to be all things to all people. But small business owners, especially those trying to get themselves established, often try to "save money" by doing everything themselves. They sell the product, empty the trash, keep the books, file the taxes, do the advertising and promotions, change the light bulbs, answer the phone, and so forth. Unfortunately, the aspects of your business which you do not excel at will be the ones that burn you out and ruin your experience as a business owner.

Focus on your strengths. If you don't do something well, hire someone to do it for you, if possible. Your true business advantage is in doing what you do well. The aspects that are difficult for you, or are outside your area of expertise, will take too much of your time and energy. You will find yourself not enjoying your business because you are not getting to do the things you do best. Moreover, not being an expert in some areas can get you into serious trouble. This is especially true for legal and accounting matters.

Doing Your Homework

Experts say that you should minimally plan to be in business for two years before you expect to turn a profit, and some businesses will take longer than that. Because of this reality of business start-up time, it is important to develop a strong support network—not only a financial network, but an emotional support system that will provide encouragement and words of wisdom in the dark moments when things aren't going the way you'd like.

Join small business owners' networking groups, or other professional organizations, where you can learn from others who have shared your experience. Take advantage of the classes and services for small business owners offered by your local community or junior college. Many colleges or university extension services offer small business development centers which can provide input and support for all aspects of your business start up. Local chambers of commerce, or economic development groups, can also be excellent resources for small business owners.

Check in your community to see if you have local chapters of SCORE (Service Corps of Retired Executives), RSVP (Retired Senior Volunteer Program), or other organizations that provide professional support in developing and running small businesses. Written materials related to various aspects of business start-up are available from the federal Small Business Administration. There may also be special departments of your state government targeted to helping women and minorities establish businesses.

Making It Work for You

People who successfully run their own businesses report that it is the best thing they ever did for themselves. With every client, sale, or job they complete, they know they have relied on their own resources and done the best work of which they are capable. The business constantly challenges them to confront their own fears, strengths, capabilities, and needs, and to re-evaluate their progress toward their on-going goals.

These same successful entrepreneurs would also tell you that starting their business took more time, energy, money, and persistence than they ever imagined. Even the most careful business plan and most realistic attitude about business start-up doesn't account for the amount of energy and effort it requires to establish a business. Be ready to meet the changing needs and demands that confront you on a daily basis. Plan to put in the time and energy you need to get your business off the ground. As the boss, you get the rewards when things go well, but you are also the only one responsible for fixing it when things don't.

Part of your personal business plan needs to include strategies for balancing the various aspects of your life as you meet the demands of your work, your family, your friends, and other commitments. It is helpful to develop a "business buddy" (your spouse, a friend, someone in business in your field) who can help you stay on course. Through a weekly "staff" meeting, this person will help you remain accountable by reminding you of your goals and commitments to yourself. Your buddy can help you examine where you need to focus your energy.

As a small business owner, aside from your knowledge of your industry, your energy is your greatest resource. Schedule and structure your time to develop effective work habits that support your needs, as well as those of your business. As a risk taker and entrepreneur, you may be used to making things happen, but you are also vulnerable to over working. It is vital that you protect yourself from burning out or getting sick. Plan your business's growth to move slowly, and get the help you need when you need it to protect your energy and keep your business manageable.

In the press of starting and maintaining your own business, it can be easy to lose site of your career and life goals. When working for yourself, it is important to constantly re-evaluate your current situation in light of your level of satisfaction, happiness, and sense of accomplishment. Are you living the life you want? Is the course of your business supporting you in creating that life? Will it in the future? Do you want your business to grow? Why?

Temptations to veer away from your plans and goals will present themselves constantly: opportunities that involve financial rewards, but also would require you to expand your business beyond a level that is comfortable for you; opening new locations and franchises that would expand your business, but require additional management capability to run; or expanding your services into areas where you don't feel you have expertise to meet a customer's specific request. You can probably think of even more examples specific to your business or industry.

Honoring your goals and needs, and honoring yourself, is the only way to maintain your happiness and satisfaction, whether you work for someone else or you work for yourself. Being human means being vulnerable to the enticements of greed, ego, and power. It also means that we can be swayed by what others say we should be doing, or by others' demands and needs, especially when we lack clarity about what we want. But as your own boss, the decisions are all yours.

Whether considering interim employment, education, starting your own business, or other creative ways to build your career ideal, two points deserve special consideration:

1) Does this action support my needs, wants, and values?

2) Will this create the life I want, now and in the future?

Some of us follow direct paths to our dreams, and others search out a more circuitous route. How you make your journey to your career ideal will be perfect, no matter what it looks like, if at each step you can honestly answer "yes" to both of the above questions.

CHAPTER 14

Loving Your Work
· For Life

N othing worth having is worth having for nothing. It's true with relationships. And it's true with your work.

Maintaining career satisfaction over time requires an important commitment to yourself and an ongoing investment of your time, energy, and creativity. Some of the strategies you began using to find your ideal job will be vital in maintaining the career momentum you have started for yourself. Your network of resource people, your portfolio, and your involvement in professional associations can facilitate your career moves. As you develop additional skills in communication or problem solving, team building or goal setting, you will be enhancing your ability to succeed and feel satisfied in your current and future positions.

The Paper Path, Revisited

As you prepared for your work search endeavors, you assembled a portfolio of samples of your work projects, written materials, evaluations, letters of recommendation, and so forth (see Chapter 12). As you enter your ideal job, this shouldn't become a dead file in the back of your desk at home; maintaining your portfolio is an important way of reminding yourself of your skills and abilities. It can come in handy for updating your supervisor on your accomplishments when it is time for your performance review or when you want to be considered for a promotion. It is also easier to maintain a portfolio "as you go" than to reconstruct one when you are in need of sample materials for future career changes or other purposes.

Your portfolio can also have value once you are on the job. For example, as a management consultant, April's portfolio contains examples of work she has done in needs analysis, materials design and development, instruction, program evaluation, and marketing. It also includes a client list, summaries of evaluations she has received, and letters of thanks from previous participants in her workshops and provides a visual "hands-on" way to back up her verbal explanations of what she can do for a particular company. April says she knows that her portfolio has been the reason that she has been awarded major training contracts.

It's Who You Know

The list of contacts you developed as a network for your work search efforts remains a valuable tool even after you have landed your ideal job. It can provide support as you learn your new work roles; give you advice when you are faced with a challenging work situation; or help you connect with other resources (either people or information). Your contacts possess a wealth of information about current trends in the industry, as well as what's happening in the local labor market, who's hiring and who's not, what kinds of professional development opportunities to pursue, etc.

When you are new on the job, it's great to have a professional peer outside of your organization with whom you can compare notes. When you've been on the job for awhile, it's still great to have the interaction and information provided by your professional network of peers, coworkers, and friends. Make the effort to keep in touch regularly. Attend meetings of your professional association, and one other organization not directly associated with your industry. Meet people and find out what they do within their organization and in their job. Make an effort to be a resource to others who are interested in entering your field or line of work.

You can also develop an equally important network among your peers at work. As a newcomer, you have a wonderful opportunity to consult with those around you on the job, to ask for information and feedback, to find out the answers to your questions, and to learn how things really work in your new company. On days when it all seems just too overwhelming, your coworkers can be an important source of motivation.

Develop a positive team of coworkers and peers who love what they do, just like you! As you start your new job, you will establish relationships that will support and sustain you through your tenure with the company. It's important that these relationships be with peers who are as enthusiastic, positive, and motivated as you.

Avoid the office "grouch." It usually doesn't take long to figure out who it is. Avoid people who seem manipulative, withholding, or who display a negative attitude. While these folks often are the first to appear to befriend the "new kid on the block"—you—they are often just seeking an audience for their complaints and their gossip and have nothing to offer you. While they may haunt the lunchroom, or stop you in the hall, it is important to politely avoid them.

Mentors

Another vital member of your professional network is a mentor. Your mentor is someone, either within or outside of your company, who knows more about your industry than you do and is willing to share the benefit of their experience with you so that you can learn.

Mentors may be men or women, younger or older, working or retired, executives or staff. A mentor is someone who currently does the kind of job that you would someday like to be doing, enjoys their work tremendously, and desires to share their knowledge and expertise with others. They can show you the ropes and give you ideas that you never would have thought of yourself about how to tackle projects. They can introduce you to key people, provide you with objective feedback about your performance, or help you when you are in a quandary about how to handle a situation.

In short, a mentor can help you build your career future. Many mentor relationships develop naturally out of the course of your association with other staff members or professional colleagues. Others result from your requests for guidance from a person from whom you would like to learn. Either way, mentors can be an important part of your career support, and advancement, network.

One of the Team

As you begin your new job, it will take time to find your role, or niche, on your new work team. Your goal is to establish yourself as a positive, contributing member of the team, known for your supportive and collaborative approach to completing tasks. It isn't enough to quietly go about your work and accomplish your tasks. You want to be seen, and accepted, as a team player.

What can you do? Take stands only on issues of how you are treated, never on unimportant or divisive issues. Find ways to express your support and encouragement for team members. Offer suggestions for changes and improvements wisely, being careful not to compare your current employer negatively to your former.

Be a volunteer and a joiner. As your work and personal schedule allow, serve on committees, agree to take on tasks and accomplish them, or accompany your coworkers if you are invited to lunch or a social activity. If there are company teams, sign up and make yourself a part of the group. When you are talking about what needs to be done, and what has been accomplished, speak of it in terms of what the team must complete or has successfully done. Acknowledge the contributions of your team members on the project's completion.

Self-Promotion

In Chapter 6, you created a list of your skills, talents, and abilities. As you enhance your skills through classes, practice, research, and so forth, make sure you update this list and keep it current. This information should be a part of your portfolio, available for your use and reference when you are looking for a promotion, new job, or clients and customers for your business.

When you have completed a class, accomplished something new, solved a problem, or reached a goal, publicize yourself! Let people know that you have successfully completed a phase in your career and are now prepared to accept new and greater challenges in the future.

You can be your own best promotional department. Choose the self-promotion strategies that will work best for you, to help you make bosses and supervisors aware of your skills and your ability to accept new challenges. Make sure you mention your accomplishments as a part of your performance review, and insure that they are noted in the final document which will go in your personnel file. Send a memo to your boss or supervisor, updating her or him on your activities. Some employees do this as a "monthly report." Others choose to send along a note only upon the completion of major activities or projects, or when they have accomplished something of importance to their work team.

Inform the editor of your in-house newsletter of your achievements, or write a short article to be included in the next issue. If you earn a certificate of completion for your class or activity, frame and hang it as a reminder of what you have done. Create a proposal for new procedures or practices developed from your new knowledge and insight. Propose changes in your job description to reflect your new skill levels. Throw a party for yourself and invite your coworkers to celebrate your success!

Self-promotion is also an excellent tool for preparing to request a promotion or salary increase. Your negotiations can be facilitated by this proof that you are a vital, learning part of the organization, who contributes to the team in creative and important ways. Remember that not only your immediate supervisor needs to be aware of your professional growth. Your self-promotion strategies should help get the word out to key company decision makers and managers as well, so that you are developing a base of support and recognition within the organization. Your immediate supervisor may leave to accept other employment at any time, so it is in your best interest to let others know about your accomplishments as well.

What I Really Want

Along with updating your skills list, make sure you are remaining current about your needs. If the only constant in life is change, your future needs will surely be different from those you have today. Periodically spending time re-appraising your work and personal needs can help you identify where you will focus your time and energy to remain satisfied with your career. Take responsibility for communicating your needs, wants, and desires. Make sure you have clarified your standing with your supervisor, within the company, and within your area of responsibility.

A Realistic Viewpoint

There are days on the job when you can't be stopped and everything seems to go your way. You feel good about yourself, your career, and your life. Then, one day, it just seems that nothing is going right. You start to question yourself, your competence, and career. On days like these, it's important to re-establish a realistic view of your expectations about youself, your job, your boss, and your coworkers.

Say that your problem is your relationship with your boss. Your boss often is not someone you selected to have as your supervisor; and because you do not select your supervisors, they can have values, a personal style, and a personality wildly divergent from your own. Given these circumstances, it is unreasonable to expect to find bliss in every aspect of your relationship with your boss. Truly, this would be the exception versus the rule.

If you are having trouble with your boss, ask yourself if you are being realistic about what your boss actually can and can't do. When you have developed a realistic picture of the situation, you are ready to think of ways to resolve your problems or disputes. Brainstorm possible reasons for his/her behavior, for your own, and methods for getting your relationship back on track. Then, think of strategies for approaching your boss that will allow you to get your needs met (see Chapter 8).

Being Realistic About Your Co-workers

While it can be intimidating to initiate actions with your supervisor or boss, it can also improve your relationship and get things back on track if you seem to have lost your momentum. The same can be true for your peers and co-workers.

Many of the same dynamics which may interfere in your relationship with your boss are true with co-workers as well. As a team, you need to work closely together and it is important to have realistic expectations about your co-workers. Your work team probably represents a broad variety of values, needs, skills, styles, work ethics, and personalities, and you need to understand their differences—with you and with each other. You will have to develop strategies for communicating with your peers, sometimes around the differences, to compensate for the variations that do exist.

In a situation where the communication just doesn't seem to be working with someone, examine your perceptions of the situation. The first step in trying to resolve situations is a personal effort. If your individual approaches don't result in change, it is time to develop ideas for working together with your peers and co-workers to impact the situation. Build a coalition. Form your strategies for making change together, and negotiate changes in your treatment on the job.

Being Realistic About Yourself

Probably the most important person to have realistic expectations for is yourself. As you begin to learn your new job, cut yourself some slack and ease up on striving for perfection. Allow yourself to adopt a "learning mentality" as you become familiar, and then comfortable, with new equipment, procedures, personalities, and expectations. Give yourself permission to ask for help, and give up feeling embarrassed when you need help to figure out something new on the job.

For instance, on Lorna's first day in her new office, although her past work experience had provided her with a high degree of skill on DOS-based computer systems, she discovered she would now be using a Macintosh computer system. Lorna's new employer's first request was to complete an important document—a project Lorna *knew* she could complete on a DOS computer in 30 minutes, but which took her 10 times as long on a computer system she had never used.

Lorna felt embarrassed and humiliated at what she felt was her incompetence. She approached her supervisor with the document, apologizing for the delay. Secretly, she was convinced her slow, weak performance would result in the end of her new job. Luckily, her boss had more realistic expectations about Lorna's learning process than she had for herself. With practice, Lorna soon became as quick and capable on her new computer system as she had been on her old one.

Give yourself at least six months to get to know your job. The excellent skills, talents, and abilities that got you the job will see you through this early learning period, and you will be competent again. Realistically, you are not going to be worth as much in your new career field. You won't have the level of knowledge and expertise you have developed in your current industry. You won't have the experience. And, because of these, you won't qualify for the same level of income. It will take awhile in your new environment to reach your full capacity, but you will get there. Keeping a realistic appraisal of your progress helps ease the transition to your new job.

Realistic expectations of yourself, your new job, your peers, and your supervisor are an essential part of a successful transition into a new working situation. They continue to be essential for maintaining your satisfaction over the years of your career. Don't put all of the blame for the rough days on yourself, or on others.

A Wrench in the Works

In spite of our best intentions and strongest efforts to avoid problems, they arise. Something slips through the cracks, something doesn't get done right or on time, someone is confused, or things just get fouled up. The specifics of the problem really aren't important, but how you resolve the situation is.

The best strategy for resolution is to solve problems as they come up. Ask questions, listen carefully, and get clarification on points that seem vague or inappropriate. When confronted with behavior that seems out of character, look for alternative explanations and check out your assumptions or biases. Ask yourself, "What can I do about this?" and accept that you can change your own reactions and behaviors, but cannot impose change on others.

Solving problems as they come up is important for cultivating and retaining a positive work environment. As you consider your best course of action for solving a problem, ask yourself what actions are in your own best interest and what supports a positive environment for you. Your goal is turning the resolution of a problem or conflict into a "win-win" situation for yourself and others.

Conflict and the need to confront others are areas of communication that most women find difficult, if not impossible. As girls we are taught the importance of being "nice," of getting along with others, being popular, and saying the right thing to keep people happy. As adults, these skills make us excellent at collaboration. We can think in creative and supportive ways of how to build a cooperative work team. We can think of solutions to problems that allow both sides to win. Women naturally create relationships and teams.

Current trends in management theory indicate that effective work teams operate in a collaborative atmosphere, where communication is centered on team building and support. This is diametrically opposed to the traditional, "top down," authoritative style of most managers, of most men. Women have a natural advantage in these areas. But in situations that require a confrontation, we are much less skilled than our brothers. Men learn competition and learn to confront challenges, head on. They learn to deal with differences of opinion, arguments, and confrontations without taking it personally.

In the workplace, women must learn to adapt their communication styles to include both collaborative and confrontational skills. Our challenge is in learning to be direct about what we want and what we need to achieve our goals. A clear, direct approach often saves time and energy, since we are not spending hours devising elaborate schemes which may not even end in our desired result.

The Winds of Change

It's been said that the only thing you can rely on is change. Things and ideas, people and circumstances are always in a whirl around us. In the workplace, we are faced with mergers, buy outs, expansions, lay-offs, downsizings, and numerous other changes that influence how, where, with whom, and under what conditions we work.

Workplace analysts now say that we need to plan for at least ten transitions in our career lifetimes. It's hard to imagine making that many career changes, but it is vital that we be prepared to make these changes, or risk career stalls, unemployment, or obsolescence.

As we look at our work today, it's difficult to project how the tasks, environment, or working conditions might shift so dramatically in such a short period of time. But consider for a moment the monumental impact of technology in the workplace over the last twenty years. Computerized systems have allowed companies to eliminate whole sectors of their work force, wiping out job titles right and left. Faxes, modems, satellite connections, cellular phones, miniaturization, and other technological wizardry have refocused our picture of doing business.

A major consumer products manufacturer used to have customer service offices, employing hundreds of people, in a variety of locations all over the country. Because of computers, modems, faxes, and enhanced telephone systems, they have now consolidated these offices into fewer locations, staffed by less employees, who field calls from all over the world. Over 1,000 jobs were eliminated because of technology.

A national food distributor now provides on-site computer terminals which are linked electronically to the distribution warehouse, allowing customers to do their own product ordering. In addition, the sales force has been issued hand-held computers which enable them to place orders in virtually any location. This technological advance has allowed the company to reduce their customer service and sales representative staff, which used to visit customers and personally take orders.

Even the die-hard American auto industry has experienced change. Robotics technology has forever changed the production assembly line. Detroit car makers downsized staff dramatically as the result of installing robots on the line to perform spot welding and other simple assembly tasks. One mechanical worker can replace as many as ten human workers.

And technology is only part of the picture. Global competition, corporate restructuring, changes in team management philosophy concepts, changing work force demographics, enhanced mobility, and a variety of other workplace changes influence, and will continue to influence, dramatic transitions on the job.

The only way to successfully survive in this kind of volatile market is to be open to learning, excited about taking on new challenges, and prepared for transition. Readiness begins within yourself as you examine your attitude toward change and open your mind to new ideas, policies, styles, and approaches in the workplace.

Updating and maintaining your work skills to keep pace with your industry prepares you for change. By attending classes and workshops, you can remain abreast of the latest trends and ideas which influence and shape your work. You can learn to operate new equipment or integrate new procedures into your work day. You can meet people who work in all aspects of your industry, allowing you to learn of the methods and approaches used to solve problems and get the job done in other companies. These methods and approaches can then be incorporated into your own company.

Be involved in your work beyond the tasks and duties listed on your job description. Ask to do new projects, or to be included on teams in your workplace that are tackling tough problems and seeking solutions. Offer suggestions for improvements in procedures or work scheduling that show your initiative and allow you to express your creativity and knowledge.

Keep your options open, committing yourself to career moves that enhance your ability to grow and take care of yourself as change happens around you. Know yourself. Know your skills and abilities. When you can see your unique package of skills, talents, and abilities in this way, beyond job titles and specific industries, you start to have a sense of how you could transfer to other jobs, locations, or employers. Seeing yourself as a valuable commodity in the job market enhances your feelings of power and control over your career options and choices, making you a master of change, as opposed to being mastered by change.

An Inside Job

Not only must we respond to changes in the world around us which influence our career options and choices, but we must also be aware of the changes within. It's important to re-examine your beliefs and work attitudes. Job security, the ability to stay with one company for life, is quickly becoming a thing of the past. Workers today are not guaranteed employment in return for satisfactory, or even excellent, performance. As an employee, you are called upon in these times to be loyal to your employer, but even more loyal to yourself.

Life in the Balance

Life is never static. Our days run together in a dynamic process, some moving slowly, some flashing by with amazing speed. And each day, a different aspect of our life seems to demand our attention. Our family. Our job. A friend. Our health. Even the little things, like the laundry and doing the dishes, tug at our attention. Each day it seems we are considering and weighing our priorities, and are often borrowing time from one important issue or responsibility to respond to a crisis or immediate need in another.

Consider this scenario: It's early in the morning, and you are planning an important sales presentation as you take your morning shower. You feel the pressure, you know it's one of the most important presentations of your career. And you are ready to meet the challenge. As you dress, one of your children comes to the bedroom door, in tears. She has a sore throat and a fever. Suddenly, your plans for the morning are in chaos, and you have to think quickly about how to handle your child's, your own, and your company's needs.

Planning and organizing are important aspects of being prepared to meet life's challenges. But we also need to develop skills in responding quickly to crises, opportunities, deadlines, and other needs. Women are particularly challenged in this role as they move into the workplace and take on more and more responsibilities.

To Everything There is a Season

You have many years to define, and then achieve, your own brand of success. At some times in your week, year, or life, your career may take priority. At other times, the needs of your children or parents may demand your full attention. Sometimes your spiritual, creative, and emotional needs have more of your energy. Allow yourself to experience the give and take of these priorities, and include strategies for addressing them in your week, month, year, and lifetime. In the highwire act of life, you will sometimes lean to the left, and sometimes to the right, but your goal is to stay on the wire by being flexible enough to adapt.

We close this final chapter with our best wishes to you for a happy and rewarding career and offer you kudos for taking the first steps on your personal journey to greater career satisfaction!

We hope that your trip with us has been informative, challenging, worthwhile... and fun! Let us leave you with this final sentiment from Agnes Whistling Elk.

*If a woman makes an act of power, she's created
something like a work of art. It changes her forever.
It gives her new vision on this Mother Earth, teaches her
to see. Teaches her to know what she feels and teaches
her to feel what she knows. When this happens, she
can recreate herself.*

AGNES WHISTLING ELK

CHAPTER 15

Resources:
What Else Is There?

Careers

The Complete Job Search Handbook, by Howard Figler. New York, Henry Holt and Company, Inc. 1988.

Composing a Life, by Mary Catherine Bateson. New York, Penguin Group. 1989.

Congratulations! You've Been Fired, by Emily Koltnow and Lynne S. Dumas. New York, Fawcett Columbine. 1990.

The Damn Good Resume Guide, by Yana Parker. Berkeley, Ten Speed Press. 1989.

Do What You Love, The Money Will Follow, by Marsha Sinetar. New York, Paulist Press. 1987.

Downsizing, by Amy Saltzman. New York, Harper Collins. 1991.

Guerrilla Tactics in the New Job Market, by Tom Jackson. New York, Bantam Books. 1991.

The Job Sharing Handbook, by Barney Olmsted and Suzanne Smith. Berkeley, Ten Speed Press. 1990.

The Lotus and the Pool, by Hilda Lee Dail, PhD. Boston, Shambhala Publications, Inc. 1983.

Shifting Gears: Mastering Career Change, by Carole Hyatt. New York, Simon & Schuster/Fireside. 1990.

Wishcraft, by Barbara Sher with Annie Gottlieb. New York, Ballantine Books. 1983.

Work of Her Own, by Susan Albert, PhD. New York, Thatcher/Putnam. 1992.

Work With Passion, by Nancy Anderson. New York, Carroll & Graf Publishers, Inc. 1984.

Working Ourselves to Death, by Diane Fassel. New York, Harper Collins. 1990.

Childhood

A Journey Through Your Childhood, by Christopher Biffle. Los Angeles, Jeremy P. Tarcher, Inc. 1989.

Healing the Child Within, by Charles L. Whitfield, M.D. Pompano Beach, Florida, Health Communications, Inc. 1987.

Self-Parenting, by John K. Pollard, III. Malibu, California, Generic Human Studies Publishing. 1987.

Professional Development

A Few Good Women: Breaking The Barriers To Top Management, by Jane W. White. New Jersey, Prentice Hall. 1992.

Breaking The Glass Ceiling, by Ann Morrison, et al. New York, Addison-Wesley Publishing Co. 1992.

Developing a Twenty-First Century Mind, by Marsha Sinetar. New York, Ballantine Books. 1991.

Dual Career Couples, by Stoltz and Loike. American Counseling Association, (703) 823-9800.

The Female Advantage, by Sally Helgesen. New York, Double Day/Currency. 1990.

Love And Profit, by James A. Autry. New York, William Morrow and Company, Inc. 1991.

No-Fault Negotiating, by Len Leritz. Portland, Oregon, Pacifica Press. 1987.

Soar With Your Strengths, by Donald Clifton and Paula Nelson. New York, Bantam/Delacorte. 1992.

The Seven Habits of Highly Effective People, by Stephen R. Covey. New York, Simon & Shuster. 1989.

Surviving Corporate Transition, by William Bridges, PhD. New York, Doubleday. 1988.

Take This Job and Love It, by Dennis Jaffe, PhD. and Cynthia Scott, PhD., MPH. New York, Simon & Schuster/Fireside. 1988.

Teaching the Elephant to Dance, by James A. Belasco, PhD. New York, Crown Publishers, Inc. 1990.

Working With Men, by Beth Milwid, PhD. Hillsboro, Oregon, Beyond Words Publishing, Inc. 1990.

Zapp! The Lightning of Empowerment, by William C. Byham, PhD, and Jeff Cox. New York, Fawcett Columbine. 1988.

Business Development

Growing a Business, by Paul Hawken. New York, Simon & Schuster. 1987.

Honest Business, by Michael Phillips and Salli Rasberry. New York, Random House. 1981.

In Business For Yourself, by Bruce Williams with Warren Sloat. Maryland, Scarborough House. 1991.

Marketing Your Service, by Jean Withers and Carol Vipperman. Vancouver, Canada, Self-Counsel Press. 1987.

The Popcorn Report, by Faith Popcorn. New York, Bantam Doubleday Dell Publishing Group, Inc. 1991.

Personal Development

A Woman's Worth, by Marianne Williamson, New York, Random House. 1993.

The Beauty Myth, by Naomi Wolf. New York, Anchor/Doubleday. 1992.

Between Women, by Luise Eichenbaum and Susie Orbach. New York, Penguin Books. 1987.

Burn-out—The Cost of Caring, by Christina Maslach. New Jersey, Prentice-Hall. 1982.

Chop Wood, Carry Water, by Rick Fields, with Peggy Taylor, Rex Weyler and Rick Ingrasci. Los Angeles, Jeremy P. Tarcher, Inc. 1984.

The Courage To Heal, by Ellen Bass and Laura Davis. New York, Harper & Row, Publishers. 1988.

The Dance of Anger, by Harriet Goldhor Lerner, PhD. New York, Harper & Row Publishers, Inc. 1985.

The Dance of Deception by Harriet Goldhor Lerner, PhD. New York, HarperCollins Publishers. 1993.

Feel The Fear and Do It Anyway, by Susan Jeffers. New York, Fawcett Columbine. 1987.

Getting Unstuck, by Dr. Sidney B. Simon. New York, Warner Books, Inc. 1988.

Healing the Shame That Binds You, by John Bradshaw. Deerfield, Florida, Health Communications, Inc. 1988.

Megatrends for Women, by Patricia Aburdene and John Naisbitt. New York, Villard Books. 1992.

Men are from Mars, Women are from Venus by John Gray, PhD. New York, HarperCollins Publishers. 1992.

The New Leaders, by Ann M. Morrison. San Francisco, Jossey-Bass. 1992.

Perfect Women, by Colette Dowling. New York, Summit Books. 1988.

Risking, by David Viscott, M.D. New York, Pocket Books. 1977.

Seven Kinds of Smart, by Thomas Armstrong. New York, Penguin Books/ Plume. 1993

Success Trap, by Dr. Stan J. Katz and Aimee E. Liu. New York, Bantam Doubleday Dell Publishing Group, Inc. 1990.

Transitions, by William Bridges. Menlo Park, California, Addison-Wesley Publishing Company. 1980.

Women and the Blues, by Jennifer James, PhD. San Francisco, Harper & Row. 1988.

Women Who Run With the Wolves, by Clarissa Pinkola Estes, PhD. New York, Ballantine Books. 1992.

Women's Reality, by Anne Wilson Shaef. San Francisco, Harper & Row. 1985.

You Just Don't Understand, by Deborah Tannen, PhD. New York, Ballantine Books. 1990.